CHURCH FAMILY GATHERINGS

CHURCH FAMILY GATHERINGS

PROGRAMS & PLANS

Edited by
Joe H. Leonard

Judson Press ® Valley Forge

Library of Congress Cataloging in Publication Data

Main entry under title:

Church family gatherings.

   1.   Church work in families.   2.   Family—Religious
life.   I.   Leonard, Joe.
BV4438.C48   259   78-9548
ISBN 0-8170-0809-8

CONTENTS

INTRODUCTION

"One generation shall laud thy works to another, and shall declare thy mighty acts"
— *Psalm 145:4 (RSV)*

About This Book

What is this book about? It's about caring, sharing, learning, having fun, and praising God across the generations. It's a book for the whole church family from preschoolers to great-grandparents. It's thirty program designs—use tested in local churches—for times when the whole church family gathers together. Here you will find program ideas for church family nights, for fellowship meals, and for holiday celebrations. There are program designs for special study emphases, involving all the generations in your church:

- mission study
- Bible study
- learning about important issues
- becoming better communicators
- exploring the meaning of "family."

The Values of a Church Family Gathering

Sometimes congregations talk about being "family centered" when in fact they contribute to generation gaps and isolation of persons by segregating singles from marrieds, parents from children, youth from adults. Congregations *can* become extended families when there are opportunities for people to get to know one another personally. Knowing a child or youth as a person means more than knowing one as so-and-so's child or someone's wife or husband. It means building relationships and sharing special moments together. Today a significant number of families are highly mobile, far from relatives, and feeling the need for the multigenerational nurturing a local church family can provide. Single persons need to be related to families, and families need to include the presence of single persons. Church family gatherings can help that to happen. The Christian church has more potential than any other institution for bringing the generations together and building a family feeling among them. We *are* members of one another!

Using This Book

Church Family Gatherings is written for the planners of church programs:

- fellowship chairpersons
- pastors
- family life chairpersons
- women's and men's fellowship leaders
- program planning committees of all kinds
- families responsible for a church family night program.

Individual leaders working alone or leader teams working together will be able to use the program ideas outlined here:

- to plan a program for the whole church,
- to introduce a new twist to a traditional congregational event,
- to start the congregation thinking about all the generations in the church family.

The program plans in this book can be used for an intergenerational summer church school, a series of Sunday evening intergenerational learning events, a school of missions for the whole church family, or as a resource in the church school, offering an opportunity for the generations to come together from time to time for learning and fun.

Some General Guidelines

Working with intergenerational groups requires something extra. Leaders will want to be aware of the variety of needs and abilities of the different generations:

- Children need activity and opportunities for creative expression in order to learn.
- Adults are sometimes uneasy at first with learning by doing and with creative activities.
- Youth are concerned not to appear "childish."

- Adults tend to talk in abstractions.
- Children are limited in their ability to think and talk abstractly.
- Youth are bored by too much "adult" talk.
- Adults need practice in listening openly and carefully to children and youth.
- Leaders are responsible for setting a climate where everyone's contribution is valued.

The programs outlined here provide activities in which all ages can join together comfortably. The directions given for sharing experiences and creations affirm the dignity of each person. An action-reflection method is the rule: doing and then talking about what was done.

If the concept of intergenerational learning is new to the congregation, it is helpful to emphasize the *church family* as a caring, sharing body when interpreting the concept to the congregation. The values of knowing one another as persons in the church family can be lifted up. Publicity needs to give a good description of what the intergenerational event will be like. Preparing the church family for the event is important.

A good way to begin introducing activity and sharing across the generations is with a lighter experience, perhaps one of the holiday programs. Or, introduce the concept by using one of these programs in a setting where the congregation is accustomed to being together with all generations present. Building on happy traditions from the past is a good strategy to keep in mind.

In reality, the church has always been an intergenerational, extended family. What the programs in this book do is help the busy, age-segregated church family come together again for learning, fellowship, fun, and worship.

As You Plan

When you have chosen a program from these pages, read it over carefully and then consider:

1. Who will come? Who will be there? Try to envision the participants.

2. Next, identify the leadership needed. Will you be the leader, or are there others to work with you? What skills does the program design require?

3. After that, consider the place where you will hold the event and the time you will have for it. What adaptations of the program will you need to make? A written outline of the program as you and/or others will lead it is a good idea.

4. The last steps you will need to take in planning are publicity (most of the programs outlined here offer some suggestions for publicity) and gathering the needed materials.

5. Then, after the event, be sure to evaluate it. How was this church family gathering received? Did it build up the church family in love? Did it help the generations to know each other? What will you do differently in the future? What would be a good program to do next time?

A Final Word

Church Family Gatherings is designed both to bring a new dimension to traditional church events and to stimulate congregations to move in some new directions. Your evaluation of this resource book is important to us. Let us hear from you. Write Family Life Education, Board of Educational Ministries, American Baptist Churches in the U.S.A., Valley Forge, PA 19481. Well-planned intergenerational church family gatherings can be experiences in which persons come first; the varied members of the faith community discover their wholeness; everybody participates; persons learn from one another and enjoy one another; and the Body of Christ is built up in love.

LOVE GOD, SELF, AND OTHERS

by W. Berkeley Ormond

GOAL: To identify specific ways in which God touches and uses my life.

INTRODUCTION

This experience is based upon John 6:1-13. Persons are invited to examine their unique gifts to the point where they can share that uniqueness openly with others.

PREPARATION
You will need:

1. An hour
2. A large room with table space where persons can work individually
3. Individual copies of the Personal Awareness Chart
4. Three pipe cleaners per participant
5. Masking or transparent tape
6. Felt-tip markers or pencils
7. Three tennis or golf balls
8. One leader/facilitator

Things to do ahead of time

1. Prepare enough copies of the Personal Awareness Chart so that each person will have one.
2. Fill in a sample Personal Awareness Chart with the pipe-cleaner symbols, etc.
3. Write instructions for the Personal Awareness exercise on newsprint large enough to be seen by everyone participating.

Publicity

In the monthly church newsletter and/or bulletin, use the question "Want to discover your uniqueness?" Give the date and time of session.

PROCEDURE AND TIMING
Opening the gathering (15 minutes)

1. Prayer
   God, our Father,
   Give us each miraculous eyes to see more clearly:
   eyes by which to see you,
   eyes by which to see others,
   eyes by which to see ourselves.
   With excitement and anticipation
   we pray in Christ's name. Amen.
2. Bible Study
   - Mark one tennis or golf ball "Philip," another "Andrew," and the third "boy." After reading the Scripture passage, place the three balls in the center of the group.
   - Invite persons, one at a time, to pick up one of the balls and "become" that person for the moment. Ask each one to explain why he or she played the role the way he or she did in the biblical story.
   - Place the ball back and invite someone else to share in this way.
3. Two Questions
   Ask the group: What did the boy with the fishes and loaves do? What did his gift allow Jesus to do?

Developing the experience (20 minutes)

1. Give each person three pipe cleaners, some masking/transparent tape, a pencil, and a copy of the Personal Awareness Chart.
2. Invite each person to fashion a symbol out of the pipe cleaners for each of the "Important Facts About Myself" on the Awareness Chart and attach these symbols to the chart with tape.
3. Show the chart you have already completed. Ask each person to fill in the appropriate spaces for each symbol they have made.
   - Parents will want to help small children with this.
4. Have a time of intergenerational sharing (20 minutes).
   - Divide into intergenerational groups of approximately six persons.
   - Invite persons to share any or all of their Personal Awareness Chart.
   - After all sharing has been completed, invite

persons to go to one another's charts and initial any part of that chart which they wish to affirm with that person. Example: A person may have fashioned a music note symbol. If this ability is recognized by someone else, encourage each to affirm it with his or her initials.

Closing the experience (5 minutes)

- Assemble in a circle.
- Close with a prayer of your choice, or you may use this one:

  God of peace!
  God of giving!

Show us the gift we should seek.
Show us the gift we must try to give.
Show us the gift we must keep.
Show us the gift you have given.
Make us what you want us to be . . .
  to you,
  to others,
  and to ourselves. Amen.

W. Berkeley Ormond is Pastor of the Cedar Hills Baptist Church of Portland, Oregon.

A PERSONAL AWARENESS CHART		
Important Facts About Myself	**Ways God Gives Me Life in This Area**	**Ways I Share My Life with Others**

"O BLESS THE LORD, MY SOUL!"

by W. Berkeley Ormond

GOAL: To identify and celebrate the ways God's love reaches us.

INTRODUCTION

This session is based on Psalm 103. Persons are invited to respond in gratitude to God whose love blesses (fulfills) us. This session enables participants to share personal understandings of God's blessings.

PREPARATION
You will need:

1. An hour
2. A large room where tables can be spaced about for each group of six or so
3. Magazines, glue, scissors, felt-tip markers or pencils, butcher paper or newsprint, construction paper for name tags, tape and/or pins
4. Record player and a recording of *Godspell,* hymnbooks, and a musical instrument
5. One leader is adequate, but a team of three leaders will find it easier to keep in touch with the small groups.

Things to do ahead of time

1. Make name tags by cutting 8½" x 11" construction paper in thirds.
2. Write all instructions on several pieces of newsprint so that the small groups can easily see them as they work around the room.
3. Make a sample collage.
4. Set up the room.

Publicity

On posters or in a mailing or bulletin insert, describe the program and use this statement for completion, "Of all the benefits or blessings I have received, I consider _____ perhaps the greatest."

PROCEDURE AND TIMING
Opening the gathering (15 minutes)

1. Have "O Bless the Lord" from *Godspell* playing on the record player.
2. As people arrive, let them make name tags according to these instructions, posted on newsprint:
   (*a*) Write your name in BIG letters at the top of the tag.
   (*b*) Under your name, write answers to this question: "If I were God, I would give three blessings in this order. . . ."
      1. _____
      2. _____
      3. _____
   (*c*) Readers and writers help nonreaders and nonwriters.
3. Gather the entire group and read Psalm 103. Announce the theme "O Bless the Lord, My Soul." Share the purpose for the session: to think together about the many ways God's love reaches us, and to celebrate the ways God blesses us.
4. Sing the hymn "Praise, My Soul, the King of Heaven," which is based on Psalm 103. An alternate hymn could be "Praise to the Lord, the Almighty."

Developing the experience (30 minutes)

1. Divide into groups of six with two adults, two youth, and two children in each group if possible. You may need to make the groups larger or smaller by one person. Avoid having only one child or youth in a group of adults. Parents may accompany a child of less than eight years. Each group chooses a table where participants can work.
2. Invite the small groups to share their name tags briefly, about a minute a person.
3. After no more than ten minutes, call everyone's

attention to the posted directions for making a group collage:

"As a group, make a collage using the magazines provided. The collage should contain *three major areas:*

a. Ways God's love has touched me through earth.

b. Ways God's love has touched me through persons.

c. Ways God's love has touched me through organizations/institutions.

Design the collage so these areas are evident. Be sure everyone has a chance to contribute."

- Describe what a collage is: a collection of pictures and/or words giving a message.
- Encourage persons to talk and share about the contributions they are making to the collage in keeping with the theme and assigned task at the moment.

Closing the experience (15 minutes)

1. Have all groups either tape their collages to the walls or lay them out on the floor.
2. Invite the small groups to tour the room and observe the other collages.
   - Encourage the groups to discuss together what they see as they tour.
   - What are some things that are special about each of the collages?
3. After no more than ten minutes, call the entire group together in a large circle.
   - Invite persons to share *new* ways they have discovered God's love touching them through this experience.
   - After each person has shared, let the group respond, "Bless the Lord."
4. Close either with the Doxology or this benediction:
   Lord God,

   > whatsoever things are pure,
   > whatsoever things are lovely,
   > whatsoever things are of good report,

   help us to think on these things, and we will claim your promise that the "God of peace will be with us!" Amen.

W. Berkeley Ormond is Pastor of the Cedar Hills Baptist Church of Portland, Oregon.

"RENEW THY CHURCH, HER MINISTRIES RESTORE!"

by W. Berkeley Ormond

GOAL: To identify specific ways in which the local church is meaningful to persons.

INTRODUCTION

This session is based upon Matthew 16:13-19. Participants will be invited to examine their local church and express openly the contributions the church makes to their lives.

PREPARATION
You will need:

1. Butcher paper, masking tape
2. A rock
3. A felt-tip marker
4. Play dough
5. Small dowels or large toothpicks
6. One leader

Things to do ahead of time

1. Mix the play dough, enough for each group of approximately six persons:
   - 2 cups water
   - 2 cups flour
   - 1 cup salt
   - 4 tablespoons oil
   - 4 teaspoons cream of tartar
   - Cook until it forms a substantial lump.
   - (It can be stored in a container for quite some time.)
2. Create a model of a car for display.
3. Set up a large room with a table for each group.
4. Print instructions on butcher paper; post so that all groups may see them.
5. If you use the closing song/benediction, print the words on butcher paper and affix to the wall at the proper time.

Publicity

Publicize via poster or newsletter/bulletins using a collage of cars with this statement: "BE A CAR DESIGNER: CREATE YOUR OWN."

PROCEDURE AND TIMING
Opening the gathering (15 minutes)

1. Place a rock at the center of the gathering.
2. Read Matthew 16:13-19.
3. Ask people to brainstorm in response to the question: "What are the characteristics of a rock?"
   - Ask for one-word responses.
   - Record these on the butcher paper. Example: strong, durable, odd-shaped, etc.
4. After about five minutes of fast brainstorming, ask the group to apply the list of characteristics to their local church. How is it like and unlike the rock?

Developing the experience (60 minutes)

1. Divide into intergenerational groups of six. Be sure to include children and youth in every group. Do not let any group have just one child or one youth. Some groups may need one more or one less than six. Assign each group to a table.
2. Focus attention upon the posted instructions (see step #3 below). Pass out the play dough and dowels/toothpicks.
   - Ask persons to share thoughts about their favorite automobile. Or, have them complete the statement "If I were a car, I would like to be a

     _____

     because _____ ."
3. Ask each group to design a car in play dough with the local church in mind. The car they design should express what they want the local church to be.
   - Do it as a group; encourage much sharing and discussion as the design comes into being.
   - Encourage a thousand questions within the groups if necessary to spark discussion. Sample questions:
     - Will it be a Model T or futuristic?
     - What is its fuel?
     - Who does the driving?
     - Are there any backseat drivers? Why are they backseaters?

Are there any hitchhikers? Any pleasure riders?
- Fantasize and symbolize constantly as a group as the car is being designed and put together.
- Remember, the car and everything about it should have some application to your concept of the local church.

4. Reassemble the entire group (20 minutes)
- Have each small group place its design in the center of the gathering.
- Encourage questions.
- As a large group, perhaps you would want to create a design, borrowing parts from the designs which are on display.

Closing the experience (10 minutes)

1. Share this prayer:
   Most wonderful and loving God,
      we praise you;
      we worship you;
      we thank you
         for everything you have given us,
         especially
         the
         church!
   Help us to come to a fuller appreciation of this gift and to share it.

2. Sing together to the tune of "Amazing Grace":
   One holy church of God appears
   Through every age and race
   Unwasted by the lapse of years
   Unchanged by changing place.

   O living church, thy errand speed
   Fulfill thy task sublime
   With bread of life earth's hunger feed
   Redeem the evil time. Amen.

W. Berkeley Ormond is Pastor of the Cedar Hills Baptist Church of Portland, Oregon.

Paul Schrock

CHALLENGED TO SERVE

by W. Berkeley Ormond

GOAL: To help individuals identify and assume personal responsibilities in the world through a study of "The Parable of the Final Judgment."

INTRODUCTION

This experience is based upon a study of Matthew 25:31-46, "The Parable of the Final Judgment," and reflection upon world hunger.

PREPARATION
You will need:

1. A large room and five tables
2. Five table name cards (8½" x 11" construction paper)
3. A beverage and an uncut stick of bologna or a loaf of french bread
4. Napkins, plates, drinking cups, some type of eating utensils
5. A bass drum and a tape recorder
6. Six drama masks (either tragedy or comedy)
7. "Birthplace" cards measuring 3" x 5"
8. A resource table with the following on display:
   - your denomination's hunger study materials
   - books, such as *Diet for a Small Planet* (Ballantine Books, Inc., 1975); *Rich Christians in an Age of Hunger* (Inter-Varsity Press, 1977); *Stones into Bread?* (Judson Press, 1977)
   - materials from hunger organizations, such as Bread for the World, 1235 E. 49th St., New York, NY 10017; Heifer Project International, World Headquarters, Box 808, Little Rock, AR 72203; Department of Church World Services, Division of Overseas Ministries, National Council of Churches, U.S.A., 475 Riverside Drive, New York, NY 10027

Things to do ahead of time

1. Set up tables.
2. Fold 8½" x 11" construction paper in half. With felt-tip marker, in bold letters write the name of one of the following continents on each piece of folded construction paper: Africa, Asia, Europe, Latin America, North America.
3. With felt-tip marker, write one of the following on each of the drama masks: hungry, thirsty, stranger, naked, sick, prisoner.
4. If you use the tape recorder, tape a bass drumbeat every 8 seconds; record 40 minutes worth. Each drumbeat represents one death by starvation somewhere in the world.
5. Prepare continental "birthplace" cards. The total number of cards should equal the total number of persons registered for the event. The total should be divided into cards for the various continents according to these percentages:

Africa	10%
Asia	59%
Europe	17%
Latin America	8%
North America	6%

6. Divide the bologna or bread into approximately the following portions:

Africa	3%
Asia	4%
Europe	23%
Latin America	8%
North America	62%

   Place each portion on a plate in readiness for developing the exercise.

Publicity

- On a poster or in the newsletter/bulletin, have a

picture or drawing of the world globe with this statement in bold letters: WHAT IN THE WORLD IS GOING ON?

- Take RESERVATIONS for this experience. You will need to know in advance how many will be coming so you can make the right number of birthplace cards.
- Request that persons not eat six to eight hours before the experience.

PROCEDURE AND TIMING
Opening the gathering (10 minutes)
Invite persons to share something of worldwide significance which has impressed them in the past week. Ask for a "feeling" word when they share.

Bible study and exploration (25 minutes)
1. Read the Scripture lesson, and ask the group to divide into six intergenerational groups. Strive for more than one child or youth in any group.
2. Pass out the masks, explaining that each mask represents one of the human crises in the parable. Send each group off to create a two-minute drama based on the crisis named on the mask handed to them. Allow no more than ten minutes for the drama creation.
3. Call everyone back together and let each group present its drama. Encourage the dramatists to "tell it as it is" and make the human crises they are acting as real as possible.

Developing the experience (30 minutes)
1. Each person draws a "birthplace" card out of a hat or bag. It is important that persons draw their own cards out of the hat/bag indicating the fact that it is not by anyone's design or virtue that they have been born in a certain place.
2. Persons assemble at the table bearing the name of their "birthplace" card.
3. After everyone is seated, read the percentage populations represented at each table, or give these approximate figures:

Africa	412 million
Asia	2,367 million
Europe	702 million
Latin America	319 million
North America	240 million

Invite everyone to look all around to get in touch with population sizes.
4. Ask each "continent" to send a representative to the serving area and pass out portions divided according to Step 6 under "Things to do ahead of time." Share and eat.
5. Encourage persons to look around and observe the differences between populations and food distributions. The food distribution represents the daily per capita consumption of persons around the world. Have the drumbeat going the whole time.
6. Encourage persons to share their feelings at their tables. Some suggested sentence completions for use around the tables are:
- Being hungry is like . . .
- Seeing others with more/less makes me feel . . .

Closing the experience (15 minutes)
1. Let the people remain at their tables. Help them to share their feelings. Encourage them to share ways in which something concrete can be done in keeping with Jesus' words "I tell you, whenever you did this for one of the least important of these brothers of mine, you did it for me!" (Matthew 25:40, TEV).
2. Draw attention to the resource table.
3. Form a circle and close with this prayer:
Father God,
    we thank you for life itself and for everything that
    makes life worth living:
        for the things we eat,
        for the things we do,
        for the people who love us and care for us.
But as we say thank-you now,
    we know that we do not always say thank-you
        in the way we live our lives.
Help us make these moments count
    for today
    and tomorrow
    and tomorrow. Amen!

W. Berkeley Ormond is Pastor of the Cedar Hills Baptist Church in Portland, Oregon.

"IT'S A SMALL WORLD AFTER ALL!"

by W. Berkeley Ormond

GOAL: To identify with the pain, anger, and frustrated hopes that countries and persons experience around the world.

INTRODUCTION

This session is based upon a study of Romans 8:31-39 and a simulation game about conditions under which persons live around the world. The program would be a good one for a mission emphasis. Persons will be invited to get in touch with how they might feel if they were to experience the things many people face daily in different parts of the world. Persons will be invited to explore their faith in a loving and gracious God under such circumstances.

PREPARATION
You will need:

1. Table space for small groups of four to six persons
2. Enough copies of the Survival Game for each group (See the foldout at the back of this book.) Be sure to check the list of things needed on the game. Have all of these items ready
3. Copies of words to the hymn "This Is My Father's World"

Things to do ahead of time

1. Set up folding tables.
2. Make copies of the game (Any type of reproduction process will do. You have the permission of the publisher).

Publicity

On a poster make a collage of international disasters and/or events that are life changing. In bold, black letters write WHY ME, LORD? WHY US, LORD? Give dates and the place of the experience.

PROCEDURE AND TIMING
Opening the gathering (30 minutes)

1. Ask persons to share the countries in the world from which they or their ancestors came.
2. Or, have persons share countries in the world in which they have visited.
3. Bible study and exploration.

- Read Romans 8:31-39.
- Divide into triads and ask persons to share an experience in life they may have had which, at the time, created some doubt about the closeness and/or goodness of God. Encourage them to share how they responded to that particular situation.
- Perhaps no one in that group has had such an experience. If that is the case, invite some sharing as to how it would be to face a situation so threatening that it could appear to separate one from the love of God.
4. Reassemble the group and sing: "This Is My Father's World."

Developing the experience (30 minutes)

1. Divide into intergenerational groups of four to six persons. Include children and youth in each group and, if possible, have more than one of each in a group.
2. Pass out the game. Read instructions from the game.
   - Remind the participants that since it is a game, they may need to work at identifying with the feelings of the persons in the game. DON'T LET THE GAME BECOME JUST ANOTHER COMPETITIVE GAME.
   - Encourage constant dialogue all during the game as persons "experience" what has just happened to them.

Closing the experience (15 minutes)

1. Reassemble as a total group.
2. Ask persons to share how it felt to be a "winner" or a "loser."
3. Invite persons to complete the sentence "Now when I read or hear about events in far-off places, I will _____."
4. Form a circle and either sing or pray the Lord's Prayer.

W. Berkeley Ormond is Pastor of the Cedar Hills Baptist Church of Portland, Oregon.

BIBLE STUDIES

"HEY, LOOK ME OVER!"

by W. Berkeley Ormond

GOAL: To help persons review their total stewardship responsibility.

INTRODUCTION

In this session, persons will have an opportunity to identify areas of stewardship: money, time, talent, use of natural resources, relation to the environment, and so on. Participants will do this in light of the creation story in Genesis 1.

PREPARATION
You will need:

1. Construction paper
2. Glue
3. Scissors
4. Felt-tip markers/crayons
5. Pencils
6. Copies of the Stewardship Chart
7. Tables to serve as work areas
8. One leader
9. Newsprint/butcher paper
10. Masking tape

Things to do ahead of time

1. Create a sample poster about the creation.
2. Write directions on butcher paper or have them duplicated for each person.
3. Make a sample "stewardship person." Remember, it is likely that this "person" will not be evenly proportioned.
4. Be sure there are enough individual working areas.
5. Take six sheets of newsprint or butcher paper, one for each day of creation. At the top of each write one aspect of the creation as recorded in Genesis 1:1-31. Example: day one, creation of light.

Publicity

On a poster or in the newsletter/bulletin, show a total black space with these words written boldly in white or some bright color: WHAT HAPPENED AFTER THIS? Give dates and place of the event.

PROCEDURE AND TIMING
Opening the gathering (3 minutes)

1. Ask the group to form a circle as a symbol of the completeness of God's creation.
2. Open with this prayer:
   Mighty God,
      your power fills heaven and earth—is hid in atoms and flung from the sun.
   Control us so that we may never turn natural forces to destruction,
   But guide us with wisdom and love at all times. Amen!

Developing the experience (60 minutes)

1. Bible study and exploration.
   - Read Genesis 1:1-31.
   - Divide into six intergenerational groups each of which includes more than one child and youth. Give each group one of the pieces of newsprint or butcher paper upon which you have written the six aspects of creation. Pass out felt-tip markers or crayons.
   - Give the groups 15 minutes to design a poster which will reflect how persons/society express their stewardship of that part of creation listed at the top of their newsprint or butcher paper.
   - After 15 minutes, call the groups together and have one person from each group tape the poster onto the wall and give a short interpretation.
2. Using the Stewardship Chart—
   - Give each person construction paper, scissors, glue, pencil, and a copy of the Stewardship Chart. Each person is to examine himself or herself by using the Stewardship Chart. Encourage them to do this within the first 10 minutes.
   - Now, ask each person to create a human body out of the construction paper. The body should be put together in proportion to the answers on the Stewardship Chart.
   Example: one may have a tiny head and have a big left arm. It all depends upon the answer in the "Scale of Involvement."

Closing the experience (20 minutes)

1. Divide into small groups of three or four persons. Each person should bring his or her "body."
2. Invite each person to share himself or herself. Work for stewardship honesty.
3. Close by asking all persons to place their "bodies" in the center of the room on the floor.
   - Form a circle around them.
   - Notice the various "shapes" of stewardship—the strengths and the weaknesses.
   - Invite persons to share ONE WORD which may express his or her feelings about the experience.
   - End with the singing of the Doxology.

W. Berkeley Ormond is Pastor of the Cedar Hills Baptist Church of Portland, Oregon.

STEWARDSHIP CHART

Part of Body	Signs of Being a Good Steward	Scale of Involvement			
		TINY Have not thought much about	SMALL Informed and convinced	AVERAGE Doing something about	LARGE Doing something significant about
Head	Sharing my money and possessions				
Chest	Seeing that each person has a fair share in life (food, shelter, clothes, etc.)				
Torso	Preserving nature for all species				
Left arm/hand	Taking care of resources entrusted to me (persons and earth)				
Right arm/hand	Living simply so as to consume as little as possible or needed				
Left leg/foot	Saving living beings (wild creatures as well as people)				
Right leg/foot	Leaving a good heritage for future generations				

I HEAR YOU LOUD AND CLEAR

by John and Virginia Pipe

GOAL: To define communication and to practice listening skills.

INTRODUCTION

"Lack of communication" is often cited as the cause for marital and family problems, for the "generation gap," and for the tensions and conflicts we experience in our relationships with others. Yet, we cannot *not* communicate; we are *always* communicating something, whether or not we use words. This session will focus on how to become better communicators through improving listening skills.

PREPARATION
You will need:

1. Ninety minutes
2. A large room with chairs arranged in circles of ten
3. Newsprint, Magic Markers, masking tape
4. A leader in charge of the session with a helper for each ten people
5. Three people for a role play
6. A record player and a record of CB (Citizens Band) songs (secure from a young teenager)
7. Material for name tags, pins

Things to do ahead of time

1. Precut name-tag material (8½" x 11" construction paper cut into eight pieces).
2. Enlist and prepare co-leaders and role players. Recruit a pianist for the closing song.
3. Ask leaders to choose a CB "handle" and wear a name tag as models for others.
4. Set up the room with circles of ten chairs.
5. Write on newsprint or chalkboard the definition and diagram of communication, other instructions which might be confusing if given only verbally, and the words to the closing song.

Publicity

1. Titles which can be used on posters and flyers: "I HEAR YOU LOUD AND CLEAR" or "CB OR NOT CB: THAT IS THE COMMUNICATION."
2. Pictures of CB units or of a car with CB antenna can be used as graphics.
3. An announcement can be made up in CB language to be given during announcement time at church school or in the church service.

PROCEDURE AND TIMING
Opening the gathering (15 minutes)

1. Have an album of CB songs playing as people arrive.
2. Ask arrivals to make name tags, using a CB "handle" they choose for themselves instead of their real names. Examples: Rubber Ducky, Sugar 'n Spice, First Lady. Have co-leaders prepared to help people think up "handles."
3. Encourage conversation about the "handles" they have chosen.
4. Divide into groups with five people over eighteen years of age and five people under eighteen in each circle of chairs with a co-leader in each group to help them follow instructions.

Developing the experience (70 minutes)

1. Play the Gossip Game. Whisper the following message in the ear of one person in each circle, who then whispers it to the next one, and so on around the circle. Ask the last person to write down the final message. Message: *Rod and Rita went to Red Rocks for a rock concert. Their tires were slashed and they didn't get home 'til 3 AM.* Make up your own statement if you prefer, but keep it rather short and simple.
2. When each group has finished, read the original message to the total group. Then ask each circle to report its final version. Be prepared for laughter at the fouled-up messages!
3. In five minutes of leader input, share—
   • the purpose for this session, drawing on material in the introduction.
   • a definition (written on chalkboard or newsprint)

of communication: *"Communication* comes from a Latin word meaning 'common union.' Communication means to create a *common union* or *shared* understanding with another person. It is a two-way process."

- a diagram (drawing on chalkboard or newsprint):

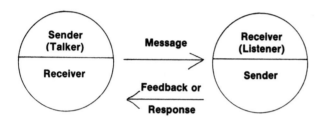

As with CB units, both units send and receive messages.

- the role of the listener: to be like a CB receiver—"switched-on" and "tuned-in."

4. Ask the role players to come before the group and demonstrate a *switched-on* and a *switched-off* listener. The spectators will need to watch and listen carefully for clues that show how the two receivers are *switched on* or *switched off*. One role player is the sender, and two are receivers. The sender takes one minute to share something new and exciting with receiver #1 and then with receiver #2.
Instructions for Receivers:

R#1	R#2
eyes wandering	eye contact
body leaning back or turned away, distant	body leaning forward, close
monotonous, bored voice	lively, interested voice
fidget	calm, alert body
interrupt	patiently listen
change subject	keep on subject

5. Draw from the group members what they saw and heard which showed being switched on or off. Add any of the above points if they are not forthcoming. Then ask the sender to share how the two different receivers' behavior affected him or her. Emphasize that in order to be good receivers, we must first of all be *switched on*.

6. Next, list on chalkboard or newsprint four ways of tuning in, using four different parts of the body:
   - listening with our *ears*
   - with our *eyes*
   - with our *minds*
   - with our *hearts*

Let's talk about and practice all four ways of tuning in. Think of it as quadrophonic listening!

7. Listening with our eyes
   - Assign each group one or two of the following feelings, which they are to act out nonverbally, using their bodies to pantomime the feeling: *excitement, upset, eagerness, unhappiness, confidence, guilt, love, fright, frustration, conceit, surprise.* If they wish, each group may choose one person to show the feeling.
   - Ask groups to take turns listening with their eyes, tuning in to guess what the acted-out feeling is.
   - After the above feelings have been demonstrated, emphasize "tuning in" to "body language," since people's feelings are transmitted through the body. Body language is part of all messages.

8. Listening with our ears
   - In order to get moving and break the tension of sitting quietly, ask everyone to stand and find a place where there will be room to move around freely. Lead the game "Simon Says" in the usual way: participants are to imitate your (leader's) body action only if you precede the action with the phrase "Simon Says."
   - Do that for a few minutes and add a variation: "Simon says, 'Raise your right *hand*,'" while raising your right *leg*.
   - How well can people listen to what your *voice* tells them, instead of what your *body* tells them to do?
   - After the game, point out that we tend to be more affected by body language than by words if the two don't match, and that body language is often more reliable than words.

9. Listening with our minds
   Moving back into the circle of ten, ask each group to play the Echo Game using the subject "Church School teachers should *never* kick anyone out of class."

   The rules are:
   - Each person must paraphrase (state in own words) what the previous speaker said before giving one's own opinion. If not paraphrased accurately, the previous speaker restates and the current speaker tries again. After a correct paraphrase, the "echo," she or he can go ahead and give her or his own opinion.
   - Listeners are to listen for *meaning*. This exercise is not designed to come up with an answer to the question; it is simply to practice listening and giving an accurate "echo" of what has been said.

10. Listening with our hearts
   - Compare the heart to the special antenna on the CB or the fine-tuning knob on radio or TV. In this exercise the focus will be on listening for *feelings*.
   - Divide into groups of two or three with a variety of ages in each pair or triad. Ask each person in the pair or triad to tell the others for two minutes about *"My Work"* or *"What I Do All Day."*
   - Listeners then suggest what the speaker is feeling and the speaker confirms or clarifies. Speakers avoid mentioning feelings directly so that listeners can practice tuning in to feelings.

Closing the experience (5 minutes)

1. Share a closing statement: Just as a CB receiver has many components which work together, each of us has eyes, ears, mind, and heart to help us do the job of receiving messages and listening. But the natural equipment God has given us must first of all be switched on and secondly tuned in to hear another person loud and clear—to create a *common union,* to communicate effectively.

2. Closing prayer: Father, help us to be like Jesus, who listened carefully to all who came to him—to Nicodemus, to the woman at the well, to the children, to the disciples, to the rich young ruler, and to many, many others. We would be better listeners to one another and also to you. Help us to switch on and tune in to you so that we might see you more clearly, love you more dearly, and follow you more nearly every day. Amen.

3. Song: "Open Mine Eyes" or "Day by Day" (words written out on newsprint).

John and Virginia Pipe live in Grand Junction, Colorado. John is Area Minister of the American Baptist Churches of the Rocky Mountains. Viriginia holds the M.Ed. in Adult Education.

Joe Leonard

COMMUNICATION

TELL IT LIKE IT IS

by John and Virginia Pipe

GOAL: To introduce a model of communication, to learn the three elements of the "I-message," and to practice sending "I-messages."

Introduction

Many psychologists emphasize the importance of emotional honesty in communicating with others. Virginia Satir calls it "leveling"; Carl Rogers stresses openness and authenticity; Sidney Jourard uses the terms "transparency" and "self-disclosure." In the Bible we are admonished to speak the truth in love (see Ephesians 4:15). One method of speaking the truth in love is what Thomas Gordon in his Parent Effectiveness Training calls the "I-message." This session will focus on becoming better communicators by learning to send both positive and negative "I-messages."

PREPARATION

You will need:

1. Ninety minutes
2. Newsprint, Magic Marker, masking tape
3. A large room with chairs arranged in circles of ten
4. A leader for each small group of ten
5. A leader to coordinate the total session
6. Bibles or New Testaments
7. Material for name tags, pins

Things to do ahead of time

1. Precut name-tag material (cut 8½" x 11" construction paper into eighths).
2. Set up room.
3. Enlist small group leaders and brief them on the session plan, familiarizing them with the "I-message" material particularly.
4. Ask people to bring Bibles; have some Bibles and New Testaments at hand.
5. Prepare newsprint instructions and the diagram of communication and the building blocks of the "I-message."
6. Thoroughly familiarize yourself with all the material in the session, so you can lead it smoothly.

Publicity

On posters or printed material, use the following: (Place the answer upside down somewhere on the bottom of the poster—"We will learn how to send 'I-messages.'")

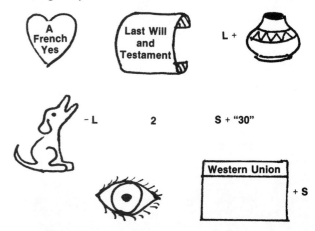

PROCEDURE AND TIMING

Opening the gathering (15 minutes)

As people arrive, have each one make a name tag with the name printed in reverse. Ask them to walk around, look at one another's name tag, and try to pronounce each other's name.

Developing the experience (70 minutes)

1. Tell the group members they've just been using one kind of code to communicate their names. In the last session they used a CB handle, which is a code name, on their name tags. There are many types of codes, including the one used on the publicity. Read to them two examples of codes. Ask the group to decipher these into a simpler message: "We do respectfully petition, request, and entreat that due and adequate provision be made this day and the date hereinafter subscribed for the satisfying of this petitioner's requirement and for the organizing of such methods as may be deemed necessary and proper to insure the reception by

aforesaid petitioner of such quantities of baked cereal products as in the judgment of the aforesaid petitioners constitutes a sufficient supply thereof." (Give us this day our daily bread.)

"You have been *jaw-jacking* (talking) with a *smokey* (state highway patrolman) in a *plain brown wrapper* (an unmarked patrol car) with a *sneaky snake* (its own CB radio).

(Don't read words in parenthesis until group has tried to decipher the message.)

2. Divide into groups of ten, each to include five adults and five children or youth plus a small-group leader. Assign each group a short saying of Jesus to put into the same code as the poster publicizing this session. Ask each group to write its coded saying on a large piece of newsprint. At the end of five minutes, participants will show their completed message to the total group and have the others guess what Jesus' words were.

3. Share the goal for the session and the following points about codes and communication:
   - We have begun to talk about codes in this session because *words* are a way of coding our experience.
   - Last session, we practiced *decoding* messages by paying close attention to body language, tone of voice, ideas, and feelings.
   - We learned that words alone do not convey the total message.

4. Share the diagram of communication:

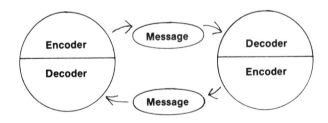

   - In good communication, the encoder sends the message as clearly as possible; the decoder listens carefully and then checks back or "feeds back" the message to make sure it has been understood.
   - In this session, we will be learning and practicing how to send a special kind of coded message called "I-messages." "I-messages" help to achieve a *common union* or communication.

5. Present the following diagram, which shows the three building blocks of the "I-message":

#1 Your feeling	#2 Describe behavior of other	#3 Effect the behavior has on you now or in the future
"I feel"	"when you"	"because"

6. Write out an example of a complete I-message: "(1) I feel very angry and put down (2) when you make remarks about my weight in front of other people, and (3) I don't want to go with you to the dinner tonight to face more humiliation." Point out that building blocks 1, 2, and 3 can be put into any order. Ask for a volunteer to demonstrate this with the same sentence.

7. In order to send an effective I-message, we need to have lots of feeling words at our fingertips to express our feelings accurately.
   - Give each group a couple of sheets of newsprint and several Magic Markers or crayons. Allow five minutes for the groups to come up with as many words or phrases as possible that describe feelings.
   - Share examples: adjectives, such as mad, glad, sad, bad; metaphors or similes, such as "mad as a wet hen," "feel like a fool," "I am on Cloud #9."
   - See which group can come up with the most feeling words or phrases. A phrase is counted as one feeling.
   - Have each group count and announce its own number.
   - Post all adjectives on a wall where they can be easily seen.

8. Because the session has been fairly intense, give the total group an opportunity to lighten up and loosen up. Tell them you want them to have some R & R (rest and relaxation) because they've been working so hard. However, instead of R & R, they will have M & M, Massage and Moan.
   - In each circle of ten, stand so that everyone can massage the shoulders of the person in front of him or her. Everyone gives and receives the massage at the same time. Participants are to moan (in pleasure rather than pain, hopefully) during the activity. Small children may need to stand on a chair to accomplish this.

9. Share a Bible story. Many Bible stories contain

good material for building I-messages. Invite the total group to listen while the story of the prodigal son (Luke 15:11-32) is read dramatically. One way to do this is with four readers, one for each character, plus a narrator. As the story is read, ask the listeners to be thinking about the father and his two sons, so they can write I-messages for them later on.

10. Each small group is then given ten minutes to come up with at least one I-message for each of the three characters, using the three building blocks of an I-message. If a group finishes sooner than the others, it may go on to do a second I-message for each character.

11. Have the groups share aloud—first, all the I-messages for the prodigal son, then the father, then the older brother.

12. Divide each group of ten into pairs with someone under eighteen and someone over eighteen in each pair if possible.

- Ask everyone to think about his or her own life and choose one positive and one negative incident or situation, either present or past, upon which to practice building an I-message. It could be something good that someone did or does for you but which you've never expressed your feelings about; or it could be a problem you continually have with someone.

- Briefly share the two situations with the partner, and help each other build I-messages to cover these situations.

- Adults can help children think through the situation and write the feeling down.
  Examples: "I'm really pleased that you vacuumed the family room without being asked. It saved me enough time that I finished folding the clothes before leaving for my meeting." "Thanks for fixing the tire on my bike. I'm really glad because I will need it for the bike hike this Saturday, and now I can quit worrying about it." "I am really mad at you for taking my toys and not returning them because I have to look all over the house to find them." "When you forget to feed and water the dog, I get really irritated because it means *I* continue to be responsible for *your* dog."

13. Share in the total group by asking for a few volunteers to read an I-message if they care to.

Closing the experience (5 minutes)

1. Review the material in the introduction section to stress the *why* of using I-messages—both for our own emotional well-being and to be clear in our communications with others. Jesus combined in himself the qualities of openness, authenticity, and transparency. He leveled with others and was self-disclosing. If we would be like Jesus, we need to be all these things, to speak the truth in love, and so freely grow into Christ.

2. Ask everyone to stand, remaining in the groups of ten; join hands; and have sentence prayers within the small group, either on a voluntary basis or going around the circle, with the co-leader for that group closing the prayer time. Since groups will be finishing up at different times, ask groups who finish first to be seated and remain silent until all small groups are finished.

3. Then join in singing one verse of "Blest Be the Tie That Binds."

John and Virginia Pipe live in Grand Junction, Colorado. John is Area Minister of the American Baptist Churches in the Rocky Mountains. Virginia holds the M.Ed. in Adult Education.

ACTIONS SPEAK LOUDER THAN WORDS

by John and Virginia Pipe

GOAL: To identify and share some of our material and spiritual values with others and to consider specific ways in which to express our Christian values.

INTRODUCTION

Dr. Sidney Simon, who along with others has introduced the educational strategy called Values Clarification, claims that a value is something that must be *chosen freely, declared publicly,* and *repeatedly acted upon* or it is not a real value for the person. In James we are exhorted to be doers of the word and not hearers only (see James 1:22-25). In this session, we will examine some of our own values and those of early Christians, and we will consider ways to live out our spiritual values day by day.

PREPARATION
You will need:
1. Ninety minutes
2. The music or record "These Are a Few of My Favorite Things" from *Sound of Music*
3. Pianist or record player
4. Newsprint, Magic Markers, masking tape
5. Paper and pencils
6. A supply of New Testaments or Bibles
7. Material for name tags (3 x 5 cards or 8½" x 11" construction paper cut into quarters), pins.

Things to do ahead of time
1. Prepare name tag instructions and a large sketch of the name tag as below:

```
YOUR NAME

Something that bugs you

Something that turns
you on
```

(a) Readers and writers help nonreaders and nonwriters.
(b) Talk to at least three people about something on their name tag.
2. To avoid confusion, write out instructions for activities, particularly those in #5 under "Developing the Experience."
3. Prepare the room by placing chairs in a circle large enough to accommodate the anticipated number of persons.
4. Prepare four sheets of newsprint, each containing at the top one of the following Scripture passages: 1 Corinthians 13; 2 Corinthians 6:3-7; Matthew 5:3-10; Galatians 5:22.
5. Write out on newsprint
   - Sidney Simon's definition of a value (see introduction)
   - examples of acting out values (for the Bible study)
   - litany response and words to the song for the closing

Publicity
1. Ask your pastor to consider giving a message on the topic "Actions Speak Louder Than Words" the Sunday previous to the session.
2. Use that phrase for posters or printed material.

PROCEDURE AND TIMING
Opening the gathering (15 minutes)
1. Have "These Are a Few of My Favorite Things" playing on the record player or piano.
2. As people arrive, they are to make a name tag according to the model you have sketched in enlarged form on newsprint and follow the other instructions.

Developing the experience (60 minutes)
1. Ask everyone to be seated. Explain that this session

will be concerned with our personal values and with our Christian values.

- Share Sidney Simon's definition of a value:
  Something—freely chosen,
  declared publicly,
  acted upon repeatedly.
- By writing on their name tags something they like and dislike, group members have already begun to declare some of their values!

2. Introduce the activity, Values Voting.
- Values Voting is done by responding to statements with hand signals:

LOVE	Raise hand, wave vigorously
LIKE	Raise hand
NEUTRAL	Cross arms on chest
DISLIKE	Thumb down
HATE	Thumb down, repeatedly pointing down

- Practice the hand signals to be sure everyone understands their use.
- Next, read down this list of items, inviting participants to Values Vote on each one:

LIVER AND ONIONS	SPINACH
FARRAH FAWCETT	HOUSEWORK
CATS	READING
HOMEMADE BREAD	REAL BUTTER
BALLET	ROBERT REDFORD
TRAVELING	CAMPING
PAUL NEWMAN	HOMEWORK
APPLE PIE	DOGS

- Add items or create your own list if you wish.
- You might ask if individuals want to call out an item to be voted on.
- Note which issues seem to divide the group most, and ask persons who voted "love" or "hate" on a particular item to share their reasons with the group.
- Values Voting is a way to become aware of how we all stand on issues that may be important to us.

3. Introduce this next step by saying "How we feel about our possessions is an indicator to us of our values." Ask everyone to imagine that his or her house is on fire.
- All the people and pets are safely out, and each person has time to go back in and take out *any* five possessions. There is no limit on size or weight.
- Ask group members to close their eyes and mentally walk through each room of the house as you name them, visualizing walls, closets, draw-

ers, cupboards—the hidden as well as the easily seen.

- Ask each person to write down or draw pictures of the five items and then put them in order from 1 to 5: 1 being the item I value most, 5 being the item I value least.
- When this task is completed, create groups of six to eight persons of mixed ages.
- Go around the group, each person sharing the #1 choice and very briefly explaining why. After all have shared #1, share #2 choices, going around the circle in the opposite direction. Groups finishing early can go on down the list until other groups are finished.
- By a show of hands, discover how many people chose items which did *not* have much money value. How often are the things we value worth money?

4. Reassemble the group in the large circle. Divide the circle into quarters, asking the ends of each quarter to pull together so that there are four circles.
- Give each group a piece of newsprint at the top of which is a passage of Scripture (see #4, "Things to do ahead of time"), a Magic Marker, and several Bibles.
- The group is to read the passage and list on the newsprint all the good qualities or characteristics of a Christian which are mentioned in the passage.
- When all lists are completed, post them side by side on a wall where everyone can see them.

5. For this step the leader will need to be very clear about the sequence of activities. Write out the instructions and go over them verbally:

a. Choose two qualities you consider most valuable from among all those posted on newsprint.

b. Write the two qualities on your name tag.

c. Walk around and find four other persons who have the same two qualities on their name tags or at least one quality you have chosen. Everyone in the group is to share at least one common quality. Be seated as soon as your group is formed.

d. As a group, choose two qualities from among the various name tags and write a statement for each quality telling how it is expressed or what it looks like in everyday life.
Examples (posted on newsprint):
Love is a father taking time to read a book to his four-year-old girl.
Long-suffering is listening to your kids' rock and

roll music without complaining.

Faith is trusting God to guide you into whatever work he wants you to do.

e. Each group chooses someone to read these two statements publicly later.

Closing the gathering (15 minutes)

1. Reassemble in a large circle.
2. Remind the group that a value is not a *real* value to a person unless it has been:
   - freely chosen from among alternatives,
   - publicly declared and affirmed,
   - acted on over and over again.

   Write the above three statements on the chalkboard or newsprint as you refer to them.
   - Point out to the group that they have been *choosing* and *declaring* their values through values voting, the burning-house exercise, and the Bible study. They have just been thinking of ways to *act on the qualities they value* as Christians.
   - Long ago a man named Jesus emphasized the importance of acting on our values. Read James 1:22-25 to the group. Emphasize that we need God's help to enable us to put our words into deeds.

3. Ask everyone to participate
   publicly declare and affirm our va
   in which we can *act on* our values ea
   lives.
   - Do this by asking each group's spokesper
     read the group's statements, one by one.
   - Invite the total group to respond after each statement as follows (written on newsprint):

     HELP US, O GOD, TO EXPRESS *(the quality)* IN OUR *LIVES* AS WELL AS WITH OUR *WORDS*.
   - After the litany, read James 1:22-25 a second time, with no comment. Let the Scripture speak for itself.
4. Close the session by singing "They'll Know We Are Christians by Our Love," or "Take My Life and Let It Be." Copy the words on newsprint so that hymnbooks will not need to be used.

John and Virginia Pipe live in Grand Junction, Colorado. John is Area Minister of the American Baptist Churches of the Rocky Mountains. Virginia holds the M.Ed. in Adult Education.

Joe Leonard

29

in a litany which
ues and the will
ch day of our
son to

HE LIVES! WE ALSO LIVE!

by JoAnn Gilmour

GOAL: To celebrate the Spirit of Jesus alive in and through persons today.

INTRODUCTION

This Easter celebration starts by recalling the stories of some of those who experienced Jesus alive after his death, includes sharing a meal, and concludes with our stories of the risen Christ of Christians today.

PREPARATION
You will need:

1. One and one-half hours
2. Church sanctuary (optional)
3. Dining room with tables and chairs
4. A meal: loaves of bread, grape juice, hard-boiled eggs with "He is risen!" written on them, cold cereals, milk, sweet rolls, coffee, tea
5. Hymnbooks; songsheets for "Every Morning Is Easter Morning" by Richard K. Avery and Donald S. Marsh
6. Costumes: three cloth squares (head covering for men); three larger pieces of cloth (shawls for women)
7. Large sheets of newsprint, crayons or marking pens, masking tape
8. A team of three leaders: Leader One plans and gets actors for dramatizations; Leader Two plans and gets helpers for the meal; Leader Three plans and enlists assistants for the sharing of our stories
9. Hymn and song leader; pianist or guitarist

Things to do ahead of time

1. Leader One: Choose three women and one teenage boy to dramatize the Gospel account in Mark 16:1-8. Choose two men (one should be a pastor) to dramatize the Gospel account in Luke 24:13-35. Gather costumes. Practice! The actors should tell the story as though it were their story!
2. Leader Two: With helpers, prepare food, color eggs, inscribe and hide them in the room; work out

details for serving tables or self-service; set tables to include a small paper cup of grape juice, plate, cup, fork, and spoon per person. Loaves of bread should be at the table where the pastor stands. Work out details for everyone to help clear tables quickly and for a minimum of cleanup following the celebration. If the cost of the meal cannot come from the church budget, place containers marked "donations for cost of meal" on each table and collect them at the close of the meal.

3. Leader Three: Gather supplies. Provide a crayon or marker for each person and one sheet of newsprint for every group of eight persons. Print these words on a large sheet of paper and post for all to see: *hopelessness, fear, envy, sorrow, anger, hurt, handicap, loneliness, depression, guilt.*

   Provide wall space for the display so that each group will be able to display its newsprint. Above this space place a sign that says: "WE BELONG TO THE EASTER PEOPLE!"
4. Music leaders: Hymnbooks and songsheets should be on tables. Order copies of "Every Morning Is Easter Morning" from Proclamation Productions Inc., Orange Square, Port Jervis, NY 12771 (or phone 914-856-6686). Cost: about 4 cents each. Practice!

Publicity

"Come to Easter on _____ at _____. Hear the Gospel accounts of those who experienced Jesus alive after his death! Share a meal. Celebrate the risen Christ of Christians today!" Include a reservation form for the meal.

PROCEDURE AND TIMING
Part I (20 minutes)

Leader One meets people as they arrive and asks them to be seated in the front pews of the sanctuary; try to create an atmosphere of waiting in silence in a dark room. At the scheduled starting time, three women and a youth come forward to tell their story (based on Mark 16:1-8). Then they remove their shawls and head coverings and urge those assembled to hear yet another story! They lead people to the dining room (dimly lit, if possible) and ask them to gather around the tables.

Two of Jesus' followers tell their story (based on Luke 24:13-35). The story leads immediately into Holy Communion. The actors remove their head coverings to signal the present. The pastor leads the people in prayer. The bread is broken and distributed to the tables (where people pass it around, each breaking off a piece). The people eat the bread and drink the juice. Then the people stand to sing "The Strife Is O'er, the Battle Done!" (Lights on!)

Part II (30 minutes)

Leader Two invites all to shake hands or embrace one another and exchange the greeting: "The Lord is risen"; (response) "He is risen indeed!" Instructions are given for the serving of the meal. Some people from each table must hunt for the eggs!

After the meal, ask all to help clear the tables (which gives people a chance to move around). The pianist or guitarist plays the tune for "Every Morning Is Easter Morning" and Leader Three and assistants place supplies on tables.

Part III (35 minutes)

The song leader invites people to join in singing "Every Morning Is Easter Morning." Perhaps one person could sing the verses this time, with all singing the chorus. Do not stop to "teach the song." If the leader and accompanist *know* the tune and *feel* the message, the people will respond in kind.

Leader Three says: "The message of Easter is that Christ lives and we also live!" The leader points to the list of bad feelings and asks people to think about times they were able to rid themselves of these crippling feelings through the presence of the living Christ in their lives. Ask them to write a word or draw a symbol on the newsprint and *briefly* share, if they are willing to do so, with each other around the tables.

The leader says: "When you hear the 'Every Morning Is Easter Morning' tune, please take your newsprint and place it under the 'WE BELONG TO THE EASTER PEOPLE' sign; also, take your songsheets and form one large circle around the dining room." If the group is too large, go back and stand in circles around tables.

Part IV (5 minutes)

Leader Three leads people in a prayer of just a few sentences incorporating words in the song and, perhaps, some on the newsprint.
Sing the song!

Leader Three says: "We've declared it; now let's go and share it!"

(NOTE: The celebration must move along or it cannot happen in the time allotted. You may have to save time by gathering for Part I outside the dining room rather than in the sanctuary.)

JoAnn Gilmour is Director of Christian Education at St. Paul's United Methodist Church in Ithaca, New York.

THE SEASON OF ADVENT

by Eric C. B. Nelson

INTRODUCTION

Advent is a very special time in the life of Christ's church. It is a period of four weeks preceding Christmas when we remember Christ's birth and think about its meaning. It is a time for Wonder; we discover again the great and glorious mystery: God has made himself known in the Child of Bethlehem. It is a time for Joy; "Joy to the world, the Lord has come!" And as we anticipate the celebration of that coming, our hearts are filled with joy and gladness. It is a time for Sharing; moved by the gift of God in Jesus Christ, we share our care and love with others, especially those less fortunate than ourselves. It is a time for Love. An old carol by Christina Rossetti said it:

"Love came down at Christmas,
Love all lovely, Love divine;
Love was born at Christmas,
Stars and angels gave the sign."

It's a love which causes us to open our hearts to others.

As a reminder of all these meanings, some Christians use a simple Advent wreath during this season. Used along with Scripture, prayer, and a carol, the wreath helps them focus on the wonder, joy, sharing, and love at Christmas. Instructions to make such a wreath and model worship services to use along with it are easily obtained from any denominational bookstore. Basically, the wreath is a circle of greenery, without ribbons or bows, around which four candles—one for each week of Advent—are equally spaced. The greenery symbolizes eternal life. The unlit candles represent the four thousand years (as calculated by tradition) the world waited in darkness for Christ. On the first Sunday of Advent, the first candle is lit. Appropriate Scripture is read, a carol sung, ending with a short prayer. On the second Sunday, the second candle is lit, and so on, until on the fourth Sunday, all are lit in a blazing witness to the One who said: "I am the light of the world" (John 8:12).

Often the Advent wreath is used in a family setting, with different members of the family taking the various parts of the service. The wreath can also be used in other intergenerational settings. The four church family gatherings which follow have been designed to be used in a local church. Each event highlights one thought symbolized by an Advent candle. The intent is to inspire all generations with the wonder of Christmas; to celebrate the joy of Christmas; to shape new attitudes of giving; and to draw all persons closer together in Christian fellowship. Each of these events concludes with a service around the Advent wreath, a service which lifts up to God the thoughts explored earlier in the event.

The four gatherings are written as a series of Sunday afternoon or evening experiences. They are each somewhat different. One is a structured evening program, while the second is a festival lasting all afternoon or evening. The third program focuses on gift making, while the fourth involves "acting out" the love of God celebrated at Christmas.

The series of Advent programs ends with a Christmas Eve intergenerational worship service.

The programs outlined in the pages that follow require careful planning and prepared leaders.

- Choose a committee to plan for these Advent programs no later than September.
- Identify a coordinator to introduce each program and keep it moving from activity to activity.
- Appoint several people (depending on the size of the crowd participating) to be small-group leaders.
- Choose persons to help with the craft activity, the music, and the closing worship services around the wreath. As a planning committee, read all four of the programs and decide how you will adapt the outlines to your church situation.

Perhaps you will want to try only one or two of these programs this year, and the others in subsequent Advent seasons. The key is advance planning. With careful preparation, you can expect a wondrous and joyous time of giving, receiving, and growing in love!

Eric C. B. Nelson is Associate Minister of the First Baptist Church of Pittsfield, Massachusetts.

CELEBRATIONS

FIRST SUNDAY IN ADVENT: WONDER

by Eric C. B. Nelson

GOALS: To experience a sense of wonder at God's gift to us in Christ. To develop fellowship and the exchange of ideas between the generations. By the end of the event, participants should be able to answer, in their own words: "What is Christmas?"

PREPARATION
You will need:
1. Two hours and fifteen minutes
2. A large assembly room with several tables
3. Materials:
   - film: *A Baby Named Jesus* (story line film by Annie Vallotton; available from American Bible Society, 1865 Broadway, New York, NY 10023); film projector and screen
   - materials for crèche (such as egg cartons, little bits of cloth, and pipe cleaners)
   - cardboard, sticks, and Magic Markers for stick puppets
   - glue, tape, colored construction paper, newsprint, or overhead projector
   - chalkboard
4. Leadership: Refer to the Introduction of this series of programs for a description of the leaders needed for these programs.
   This program requires
   - a coordinator, who will introduce the event and keep it moving from activity to activity
   - a group in the church (such as the youth group) to prepare the snack supper
   - several people to lead the discussion in the small groups
   - several people to supervise the craft projects
   - someone to lead the service around the wreath

Things to do ahead of time
1. Collect materials.
2. Order film.
3. Plan the crafts in detail and make samples.

4. Print up the words of several familiar carols, including "The Friendly Beasts."
5. Make an Advent wreath (or purchase one at a local florist).
6. Set up room.

Publicity
1. Advertise in the church newsletter and Sunday morning bulletin, either with short weekly articles or a special booklet outlining the events.
2. Posters: make one in the shape of an Advent wreath, adding another candle each week with the theme written on it.
3. Use a "Peep Box." This is a 3' x 3' box made out of plywood or heavy cardboard. There is a hole on top to peep through and a light inside. The Advent event for a Sunday would be described on the bottom of the box; so as you "peep" through the hole, you are looking directly at the ad.
4. Be sure to stress that everyone is welcome: singles, couples, and families (even those with small children).

PROCEDURE AND TIMING
Opening the gathering (60 minutes)
1. Begin the evening with a snack supper. This relaxes people and gives a good sense of fellowship. But keep the meal simple and cheap. Usually sandwiches, chips, drinks, and dessert will be enough. Try to keep the cost per person under a dollar. Otherwise families might stay away.
2. Under the coordinator's leadership, gather the group together, welcome, and introduce the evening, stating the theme and the order of events. Then divide into groups of eight. Let persons choose where they will go, but encourage parents and children to be in different groups. That way, everyone is likely to get to know people outside their family.
3. Small-group leaders, assigned beforehand, lead

their groups through the following exercise:

- Say to the group: "Let's pretend. You have a new friend. His name is John. He doesn't know what Christmas is. How would you tell him?" Write the group's answers on newsprint or chalkboard.
- Then, without leaving the small group, all turn their chairs so they can see a screen. Show the film *A Baby Named Jesus.*
- Return chairs to the original formation and help the group summarize its thoughts on Christmas by developing a group cinquain poem:

  Choose ONE word related to your subject. It should be a noun.

  Choose TWO words that describe the noun.

  Choose THREE words that are action words related to the noun.

  Choose FOUR words that are feeling words that relate to the noun.

  Choose ONE word that refers again to the noun.

  For example:
  Christmas
  Jesus' birth
  Eating, getting, sharing
  Joyous time of love
  Peace

- When the poem is completed, tape it up on a wall while the group is excused to go to the craft project. This poem will be used later on.

Developing the experience (60 minutes)

4. The coordinator directs the entire group to some tables, where the meanings talked about will be reinforced through a craft project. As people work on this project, suggest they continue to talk about the meaning of Christmas and Jesus' birth.
   Suggested projects:

   - Make a crèche. There are several easy designs available in craft books. One is found in *Teaching and Celebrating Advent* by Pat and Don Griggs. It is made out of egg cartons, bits of cloth, and pipe cleaners and could be made in an hour. Order the book from Griggs Educational Service, P.O. Box 363, Livermore, CA 94550.

   - Make stick puppets of the animals in "The Friendly Beasts" carol. Find instructions for stick puppets in any craft book, but make them at least twelve inches high, so they can be easily seen. Use them at the close of the evening, having the people who made them hide behind the piano and lift them up when their animal is mentioned in the song.

   NOTE: Be sure to make samples of the craft projects in advance.

Closing the experience (15 minutes)

1. Arrange crèches around the Advent wreath.
2. Use the cinquain poems as a backdrop for worship.
3. Sing several carols, ending with: "O Come, O Come, Emmanuel."
4. Invite a child to light the first candle. As it glows, recite in unison the phrase "With wonder, we prepare our hearts for the coming of Christ."
5. The worship leader introduces the Scripture reading by saying, "Listen to the prophets, who were filled with wonder as they thought of the coming Messiah!" Read Isaiah 9:2 and Isaiah 7:14.
6. Conclude by saying, "The prophets wondered about these things, and so have we this evening. Here is our own response as we have wondered together about the Christian mysteries." Invite members of each small group to read the cinquain poem written by their group.
7. Sing "The Friendly Beasts," using the stick puppets. (If no one chose to do this project, sing "Joy to the World.")
8. Hold hands for prayer. In an impromptu prayer, thank God for the wondrous coming of the Christ child. Pray for love and peace in our lives.

Eric C. B. Nelson is Associate Minister of the First Baptist Church of Pittsfield, Massachusetts.

CELEBRATIONS

SECOND SUNDAY IN ADVENT: JOY

by Eric C. B. Nelson

GOAL: To experience the joy of Christmas and of being together as a church family.

PREPARATION
You will need:
1. Two hours
2. A large assembly room or a cluster of several small rooms
3. Materials: the descriptions of the various activities outlined below include a list of materials needed
4. Leadership—same as for the first event

Things to do ahead of time
Gather materials, ask people to plan and staff booths, decorate room, bring Advent wreath.

Publicity
1. In addition to the suggestions made for publicizing the first event, make several "balloon trees" with "JOY," the date and time written on each balloon. A balloon tree is a pole (a six-foot dowel will do) with clusters of balloons tied to it at the top.
2. Also, suggest that people bring instruments, rhythm instruments, and kazoos for a carol sing-a-long.

THE OVERALL PLAN
- Create a carnival atmosphere with festive decorations: lots of Christmas lights, evergreen garlands, tinsel, streamers in Christmas colors, and other suitable trimming.
- Around the room set up several booths for eating and crafts. There should also be open spaces for games, a piñata, and music making. Arrrange it like a church fair.
- People will not need to come at a set time although you will need to indicate in the publicity when the room will open and close. Encourage people to come when they want, eat when they want, and wander from booth to booth, participating in the various events. Try to keep it all in one room. That will give the participants a feeling of being in the midst of joyful noise.

EATING PROCEDURE
- Sell food tickets for under a dollar. A ticket will buy a hot dog, drink, and chips, which persons can pick up at their leisure from the kitchen or a special booth. The ticket price will also cover costs of the dessert booths.
- Dessert booths: Invite families to prepare and have available for tasting Christmas desserts from other countries with recipes for those who want them. Ask for family recipes, ethnic dishes. Ask cooks to be prepared to explain any Christian symbolism the dessert may have, or any story behind it. Provide a place where people can make and bake some simple Christmas pastries. These must be easy enough to do in a short time, such as cookie cutting and/or decorating with frosting; date stuffing; a Christmas pudding to mix up; bread baking—already risen and kneaded—to be arranged into Christmas shapes. Directions for making a special Christmas pastry, Lucia cakes, can be found in *Christmas Crafts: Things to Make the 24 Days Before Christmas* by Carolyn Meyer (Harper & Row, Publishers). $5.95.

CRAFT-MAKING BOOTHS
1. Make a Christmas hat, using scissors, construction paper, and tape. Have a contest later on in the event and choose a "winner."
2. Twist wire into Christmas symbols. Dip into liquid plastic. Let dry and hang on a hanger for a Christmas mobile. Suggested symbols: dove, lighted candle, crown, star, cross, fish, bread, cup.
3. Make your own wrapping paper, decorating it with Christmas prints, stamping on designs cut from vegetables, such as a potato.
4. Make thumbprint greeting cards, using thumbprints to create Christmas designs. Write a

Christmas message on the inside of the card.

5. String art: take an 8″ x 4″ x ¾″ block of wood; cover it with red felt. Hammer in small nails in a pattern so that by adding green and metallic thread you will have a Christmas tree. Use a piece of bark for the trunk.

6. Soap-flake modeling: dampen soap flakes with just enough water to moisten them. Beat the mixture with an egg beater until it is of easy-to-mold consistency. Soap-flake modeling on paper creates a three dimensional effect when the soap dries. Sprinkle the finished product with glitter. You'll need "old-shirt smocks" for the younger children.

7. Music booth: have an Autoharp, rhythm instruments, and a piano for people to play, also books of carols and instructions for playing them on the Autoharp.

OTHER ACTIVITIES IN OPEN SPACES

1. Christmas games, especially those from other countries, can be found in Christmas books in your local library. Have several corners where such games can be played. Assign someone to direct each game.

2. Toward the end of the evening, have a piñata. A piñata is a papier-mâché, or sometimes pottery, container decorated to look like a bird or animal and suspended so that it swings freely. It is filled with candy and small toys. Blindfolded children take turns swinging at the piñata with a stick. Finally, someone breaks it open; a shower of treats causes all to scramble for the goodies!

3. Arrange a table with items to feel which were present in the stable at the time of Jesus' birth: horsehair, sheeps' wool, goat hair, a vessel to hold oil for anointing, an earthenware bowl, a wick to make a simple crude light, a candle lantern.

4. Prepare a table holding boxes containing scents that remind us of Christmas: Make holes to smell through in several brightly wrapped boxes. Included might be gingerbread, pine needles, orange rind, and peppermint.

CLOSING ACTIVITY

1. Gather around the Advent wreath. Using the piano and any instruments people may have brought, sing the first verse of several carols. Dim the lights for this and light several candles around the room. If your church has large candelabra, such as might be used at weddings, bring them in and light them. End with a quiet carol.

2. As a child lights two candles on the Advent wreath, repeat together: "We celebrate with joy the miracle of Christ's birth."

3. Let the leader say: "Listen to Luke as he writes of the shepherds' joy," and then read Luke 2:8-16.

4. Sing all verses of "Joy to the World."

5. Hold hands for prayer. Pray about joy in our hearts and touching others with that joy.

Eric C. B. Nelson is Associate Minister of the First Baptist Church of Pittsfield, Massachusetts.

CELEBRATIONS

THIRD SUNDAY IN ADVENT: SHARING

by Eric C. B. Nelson

GOALS: To develop new attitudes about sharing. To encourage the exchange of ideas among the generations and to develop fellowship. By the end of the session, participants should be able to state in their own words why we give at Christmas and will have made at least one gift for another person.

PREPARATION
You will need:

1. One and one-half hours
2. A large assembly room
3. Filmstrip projector, filmstrip *St. Nicholas,* or a copy of *The Giving Tree*
4. Materials to make the gifts you have decided upon (see "Developing the experience," #4).

Things to do ahead of time

1. Decide which story to share with the gathering:
   - "St. Nicholas" (printed at the end of this program) or order it as a filmstrip from Cathedral Films, 2291 W. Alameda Ave., Box 1608, Burbank, CA 91505.
   - *The Giving Tree,* Shel Silverstein (Harper & Row, Publishers, 1964), $4.95.
     The Giving Tree is handsomely illustrated. As you read, plan to "show it" with an opaque projector or copy the drawings onto newsprint or transparencies for an overhead projector.
2. Be sure to *practice* with the AV equipment; make sure you have extra bulbs for projectors and so on.
3. Choose several gift-making projects from the list in #4 in "Developing the experience." Secure the materials and leaders to carry out the activity.
4. Decide where to deliver the gifts and appoint a committee to deliver them. Places might include a prison, nursing homes, homes of shut-ins, hospitals, homes for retarded children, and the like.

PROCEDURE AND TIMING
Opening the gathering (30 minutes)

1. Begin with a snack supper. This time have people bring sandwich fixings to *share.* Charge 25 cents to cover the cost of bread and drink. Make a tossed salad and/or provide chips.
2. Gather the group together with words of welcome. Introduce the theme: Sharing. Speak about Christmas as a time for giving in response to Jesus, God's gift to us. Moved by God's gift, we share our love with others, especially those more needy than ourselves.

Developing the experience (50 minutes)

1. Divide into small groups.
   - Small group leaders raise two questions for reaction:
     a. What is the best gift you ever received?
     b. What is the best gift you ever gave?
   - Invite response after each question.
   - Then tell group members they're going to hear a story about someone who gave to others.
2. Reassemble as a large group to hear a story.
   - Tell the story you have chosen:
     "St. Nicholas" or "The Giving Tree."
3. Invite sharing of comments in response to the story.
   - Summarize the comments by stating:
     Giving to others is part of the message of Christmas.
   - Announce that all will have a chance to act on this message by making gifts for someone else.
   - Announce where the gifts will be going and describe the choices of gift-making activities.
4. Move to the gift-making centers.
   a. Calendars: take a 14" x 4" piece of poster board. Make it into a triangle by bending it at the 6" mark and then again at the 12" mark. Join the free ends with a piece of tape. Cover the front with a piece of felt. Make a Christmas design on

it with felt, such as an angel, a bell, a small manger scene, or the like. Glue a small one-inch calendar near the bottom. These can be bought in any stationery store.

b. Bedside bags for trash, to be used in nursing homes or hospitals: use small paper bags; decorate with Christmas decorations, such as old Christmas cards, vegetable printing, pieces of construction paper, Magic Markers.

c. Pomander balls: use an apple, whole cloves, cinnamon, ginger, yarn, and ribbon. Hung in a closet or placed in a drawer, it is a reminder of the aromatic gifts brought to the first Christmas Child.

d. Wooden toys: have someone with tools cut out several wooden toys, for example, four-inch trucks. People can sand them, glue them together, and apply shellac.

Closing the experience (10 minutes)

1. Gather around the Advent wreath.
2. Sing a couple of carols.
3. Ask a child to light three candles on the wreath. As they glow, repeat together: "We remember God's perfect gift—Jesus."
4. Say: "Listen to the story of the Wise Men, who gave in response to God's gift." Then read: Matthew 2:1-12.
5. Sing: "We Three Kings," verses 1 and 2.
6. Read the following: "The legend tells that when Jesus was born, the sun danced in the sky; the aged trees straightened themselves and put on leaves and sent forth the fragrance of blossoms once more. These are the symbols of what takes place in our hearts when the Christ child is born anew each year. Blessed by the Christmas sunshine, our natures, perhaps long leafless, bring forth new love, new kindness, new mercy, new compassion. As the birth of Jesus was the beginning of the Christian life, so the unselfish joy at Christmas shall start the spirit that is to rule the new year." by Helen Keller.
7. Hold hands for prayer. Thank God for his gifts to us. Pray for unselfishness and thoughtfulness.

Eric C. B. Nelson is Associate Minister at the First Baptist Church of Pittsfield, Massachusetts.

THE LEGEND OF ST. NICHOLAS[1]

The sun was beginning to go down behind the long row of trees at the far end of the garden as Bishop Nicholas walked up and down on the soft green grass.

"Praise be to God for this day," he said softly. "Praise be to God for the coming night. Praise be to God for a time to work. Praise be to God for—" suddenly Nicholas stopped. "I thought I heard a child crying," he said to himself. He listened, and the sound came again.

Nicholas started toward the garden gate, where the sound seemed to come from. He tried to hurry, but his old legs were stiff and the path was rough. Just as he reached the gate, which stood open just a little, he stopped. There on the ground, nearly hidden behind a bush, sat a little girl, crying.

Nicholas reached out his hand and touched her head. "Hush, little child," he said quietly, "nothing will harm you here. Tell me why you are weeping."

"I'm lost," sobbed the child. "I ran inside the gate because it was open, and when I went back to the road my mother had gone on without me. I don't know how to get home. I want my mother!"

Nicholas sat down on a bench nearby. "Don't cry any more," he said. "Just tell me your name, my child. I will find your mother for you."

The little girl looked at the kind face of the old bishop, and then she smiled. "I know who you are," she said, "you're Bishop Nicholas. You will take me home, won't you? Everyone knows you always help little children."

"Thank you, child," said the bishop. "One of my servants will see that you get home safely. But unless you tell me your name, how can I know where your home is?"

That night the family of Theodore the baker told all their friends how Bishop Nicholas had given food to their child and then sent her safely home with a basket of fruit for her brothers and sisters.

The neighbors shook their heads. "That's just like the good bishop," they said. "If he sees a child crying in the street, he always stops to help, no matter if the church is full of people waiting for the service to begin!"

"Not only children," said Theodore. "I could tell you many stories about cold, hungry people who received warm clothes and food from the bishop. I don't think he could go to sleep at night if he knew of someone who needed help. Sometimes his servants grumble because he sends them all over the city in all kinds of weather to carry his gifts to people in need."

A few months later the bells in the church told the sad news that Bishop Nicholas was dead. The people wept, for they loved the old man dearly. The poor people especially mourned his death, for he had helped them many times when they had no food or shelter for their families.

Then one of Nicholas's friends thought of a way to carry on the bishop's acts of kindness. "Meet me tonight at the church just at the midnight hour," he said to some other friends, "and I will tell you my plan. Wear a red cloak and pull your hood low over your face so that no one will recognize you if you are seen on the road."

That night the little group met as planned. "We are going to take this food to old widow Myra," said their leader, "and we will leave these clothes on the doorstep of Hans the woodcutter. He hurt his hand in an accident and has been unable to earn money to buy clothes for his children. Remember now, we are doing this in the name of good Bishop Nicholas and no one must know who we are!" And off they rode into the night.

Month after month the poor people told of finding gifts of food, money, and clothing just as they had when Nicholas was alive. Some reported that they had seen a red-robed figure leaving the gifts, but no one knew who it was, for he always disappeared quickly into the darkness.

"Maybe it is Nicholas himself," they began to say. "Maybe he is still going about just as he used to do."

As time went on, the story changed a little. "It *is* Nicholas," said the people. "He is still caring for us, just as he always did."

Years passed and the story of good Bishop Nicholas spread far beyond the city where he had lived. Many people liked the idea of helping the needy, in the name of the beloved bishop.

How surprised would be the little group of Nicholas's friends who wanted to carry on his deeds of loving-kindness if they could know how their idea has grown! At Christmas time, all over the world people give gifts of loving concern to others in need of their help; these gifts they label simply "from St. Nicholas."

¹Reprinted by permission of the publisher from *People Who Knew God* by Gertrude Priester. Copyright © 1964 by the United Church Press.

FOURTH SUNDAY IN ADVENT: LOVE

by Eric C. B. Nelson

GOALS: To discuss God's gift of love to us in Jesus. To experience God's love in our church community.

PREPARATION
You will need:

1. Two hours and ten minutes
2. A large assembly room
3. Pictures from the church school curriculum, or the play: "Listen to Christmas"
4. Felt and burlap for making group banners
5. A ball of yarn

Things to do ahead of time

1. Gather materials.
2. Set up room.

Publicity

Ask everyone to wear comfortable clothing and bring a blanket to sit on.

PROCEDURE AND TIMING
Opening the gathering (30 minutes)

1. Begin with a snack supper (keep the cost under a dollar).
2. Gather and welcome the group.
3. Introduce the theme: "Someone said that the best way to send an idea is to wrap it up in a person. That's exactly what God did: to tell us about love, he sent Jesus. God's love for us moves us to love each other. To experience an atmosphere of loving concern, in which we are open to God's love and love from each other, we'll do several exercises. These exercises are designed to relax us, to help us develop a sense of fellowship and closeness, and they are fun."

Developing the experience (90 minutes)

1. Ask all to spread their blankets on the floor and lie down, as if asleep. Then lead the group through the following exercises*:

a. Stretching: "Imagine yourself getting up in the morning; yawn and stretch; let all your tiredness out; stretch every muscle and let go."

b. Slap downs: "Stretch your left arm straight out and slap it down with your right hand from the shoulder to the fingertips and back again. Then do the same with your right arm, using your left hand. Next, stand up, and with both hands, slap down your left leg; and finally your right leg."

c. Progressive milling

• "What I'd like you to do is mill around aimlessly; *avoid* contact as much as possible with other people in the room. Don't look at them. Just act as you usually do when you're downtown, walking down the sidewalk. Try not to brush up against anyone. Avoid eye contact. As you're milling around, try to be aware of your feelings. Notice the space between you and the people around you. How does that space feel to you as you move around in it?"

• After a minute or so, let the leader say, "Now I'd like you to begin just vaguely noticing each other as you walk around."

• After another minute, "Now I'd like you to add something to this. Look into each other's eyes as you go by. While you're at it, why don't you notice what color eyes people have?"

• Allow two or three minutes to go by. "Just touch each other now as you go by—on the shoulder or something like that."

• After a couple more minutes, "Now why don't you very lightly tug at each person's ear lobe as you go by?"

• Next, "Now try shaking elbows."

• After two more minutes, "As you go by, I'd like you to face each person, put both hands on his or her shoulders and shake, just briefly. Then

*Adapted from an unpublished thesis, by George H. Tooze, entitled: "Group Exercises and the Church, an Interpretive Handbook."

41

go on to the next person and do the same thing."

d. Nonverbal greetings: "Get on your hands and knees and bump into other people. Be aware of your feelings as you make contact. Be aware of interaction that develops; show with your whole body what your responses are."

e. Shoulder rub down: "Stand in a circle (or several circles of ten to fifteen people), turn to the right and rub down the shoulders of the person in front of you. Then turn in the opposite direction and do the same."

f. Mirror: "Form pairs, preferably an adult with a child or youth. One person puts hands up, fingers out, and begins to hand-dance, moving his or her hands as if against a glass. Now, partner, with your hands about an inch away, try to keep up with the movement exactly as though you were the reflection in a mirror." After two or three minutes, ask partners to reverse roles and do it again.

2. Bring together three pairs to form small groups and sit on the blankets. Invite the groups to talk briefly about the preceding experience. Do they feel relaxed? Do they feel more like a community, feel love among the group?

3. Find several pictures from the church school curriculum that show friendship and love. Pass them out to the small groups. Ask the following questions:

• What do you like about this picture?
• How do the colors make you feel?
• What are the people doing in the picture?
• What does the artist want us to think about?

4. Then pass out pictures of the Nativity (from your church school curriculum). Ask the groups to talk about the same questions again.

• Alternative Activity: Read the play "Listen to Christmas" by Judy Smith. (Available from Contemporary Drama Service, Arthur Meriwether, Inc., 921 Curtiss St., Box 457, Downers Grove, IL 60515). This play requires no rehearsals and actively involves all ages. A narrator reads the Christmas story; the audience, divided into four groups, is asked to make the "sounds of Christmas" when pointed to (animal noises, wind, soldiers marching, and so on). Introduce the play with a few words about God's love for us and the love we show one another.

5. Let the leader share some thinking about God's gift of love.

• Relate God's love to what was experienced earlier and to the pictures of friendship, Nativity, or the play.
• End by reading the carol "Love Came Down at Christmas."

6. Introduce the banner-making activity.

a. Group Banner: Give each group of six a piece of felt or burlap 18″ to 24″ long. Create the banner by cutting shapes from smaller scraps of material (felt, print scraps, corduroy, and so on), and gluing pieces on the background. Ideas for designs can come from the Christmas story, from Christmas cards, and also catalogs from Argus, Abbey Press, and Printery House. Encourage the groups to define a theme and sketch a design first. A group banner fits right into the theme of love, togetherness, and group cooperation.

Closing the experience (10 minutes)

1. Use the banners as a backdrop for worship around the Advent wreath. Turn the lights low and light many candles. Sit on the blankets.

2. Ask a family of four to light four candles on the wreath. As the candles glow, repeat in unison the phrase "We give thanks for the good news of Jesus Christ."

3. As a sign of Christian love for one another, pass a large ball of red yarn around the group. Ask each person to wrap the yarn around his or her wrist and then pass the ball to the next person, without cutting it, so that eventually everyone will be tied together just as Christ has tied us together.

4. Sing several carols (while still tied together).

5. Introduce the Scripture by saying, "Listen to John as he speaks of God's gift of love." Read: John 1:1-5; 3:16-17.

6. Sing "Silent Night."

7. Pray, thanking God for the great love revealed in Jesus Christ. Ask for help to show that love to others, especially those in need. Ask God to fill hearts and homes with peace, joy, and love.

Eric C. B. Nelson is Associate Minister of the First Baptist Church of Pittsfield, Massachusetts.

CHRISTMAS EVE WORSHIP

by Eric C. B. Nelson

INTRODUCTION

This is an informal, half-hour, candlelight Christmas Eve service for all ages. It provides a climax for the Advent experiences that have gone before, but it can also stand alone.

For the service, light all four candles of the Advent wreath. Place in the center and light one large candle, a "Christ candle." When the moment comes to light the smaller candles held by the family groups, light them from the Christ candle.

A printed order of service would be helpful, with the words of the Call to Worship, Unison Prayer, and the Benediction included.

YOU WILL NEED

1. A worship leader
2. A storyteller
3. A reader for the echo pantomime
4. An actor for the echo pantomime

PUBLICITY

If you plan to collect canned goods, as suggested, be sure to give several weeks' notice in the bulletin, newsletter, and announcement time.

ORDER OF WORSHIP

Call to Worship (read by an adult):

Christmas returns, as it always does, with its assurance
    that life is good.
It is the time of lift to the spirit,
When the mind feels its way into the commonplace,
And senses the wonder of simple things: an evergreen
    tree,
Familiar carols, merry laughter.
It is the time of illumination,
When candles burn, and old dreams
Find their youth again.
It is the time of pause,
When forgotten joys come back to mind, and past
    dedications renew their claim.

It is the time of harvest for the heart,
When faith reaches out to mantle all high endeavor,
And love whispers its magic word to everything that
    breathes.
Christmas returns, as it always does, with its assurance
    that life is good.*

Sing two familiar carols.

Pray in Unison: And now comes Christmas. Now comes the Christ child again. May we mirror his light. May we share his life. May we return his love. Come, Lord Jesus. Amen.

Solo or Another Carol

Echo Pantomime: "We Found Him!" (printed at the end of the service outline). As a reader speaks each line, an actor "echoes" the words in pantomime.

The Christmas Story: Luke 2:1-20

Carol: Before the carol, ask the children to come forward. Then follow an old Moravian custom: the children sing the first line of the carol, and then the congregation responds with the second, and so on.

Story: Invite the children to move to the floor, around a storyteller, who then shares a Christmas story. Suggestions: *Christmas* by Dick Bruna (Doubleday & Co.) or *The Shepherd* by Heywood Hale Broun. Many stories from the church school curriculum would also be appropriate choices.

Response: Invite the children to bring forward the canned goods they have brought for the Salvation Army, Christian Social Center, or some other agency that has a "food closet" for needy people. They remain up front for the candlelighting.

Candlelighting: As "Silent Night" is played, everyone (parents will join their children) gathers around the Advent wreath. Pass a candle to each individual and family for lighting from the Christ candle. When all are lighted, sing the first stanza of "Silent Night."

Benediction (read by an adult as the candles are held): "May He settle this Christmas in your hearts so that

*Howard Thurman, *The Mood of Christmas* (New York: Harper & Row, Publishers, 1973), p. 22.

each day of the coming new year will renew the birth of Christ within your innermost being. May your lives be glorious Christmas trees, all illuminated and gift-laden for all whom God brings to the doors of your consciousness. May your whole being become a blithe Christmas carol, rising to the feet of God on strong, white wings of rejoicing and thanksgiving" (written by a Moslem for her Christian friend).

Eric C. B. Nelson is Associate Minister of the First Baptist Church of Pittsfield, Massachusetts.

ECHO PANTOMIME*
WE FOUND HIM!
(An echo action drama based on the Christmas story)

I am a shepherd boy. I guard my sheep all day.	*(Stand tall.)*
I do not let wild animals come near my lambs.	*(Hold arm up, as if with club or shepherd's rod.)*
I try to be brave and strong.	*(Shoulders back.)*
At night, my sheep come together and sleep.	
I rest, too.	*(Slump down, relaxed.)*
I rest here.	*(Point down to ground.)*
My sheep are out there on the hillside.	*(Point forward on ground.)*
Tonight, the sky is clear and bright.	*(Point upward.)*
My friends and I will build a campfire to keep warm.	*(Press arms against chest, shiver.)*
Oh, the fire is warm!	*(Hold hands out to fire.)*
The heat feels good. I'm sleepy.	*(Yawn, drop head to chest.)*
Hey! What's that bright light?	*(Put arm across eyes.)*
Listen! Someone said: "Do not be afraid!"	
But, wow! I'm scared!	*(Peek around crook of raised arm.)*
Listen! The voice says: "Christ the Lord is born in Bethlehem."	*(Cup hand to ear and pause to listen.)*
Some of the shepherds say: "Nonsense!	
It can't be the Christ!"	*(Shake head back and forth vigorously.)*
Others say: "Shall we go?" I want to go, too!	*(Shake head up and down eagerly.)*
We run down the hill toward Bethlehem.	*(Run, standing in place.)*
We run down the quiet streets.	*(Continue running in place.)*
Everyone is asleep. The lights are out.	*(Gradually—slow down to a walk.)*
Where is the baby? Where is everybody?	*(Walk slowly—look all directions.)*
Hey! There's a light!	*(Point—quicken steps.)*
But it's in a stable. That's no place for Christ.	*(Slow steps; almost stop.)*

*By Elinor Ringland, in *The Methodist Teacher*, Winter, 1970–71. Copyright © 1970 by Graded Press.

Well, let's ask inside. They may know.	*(Begin a slow walk again.)*
Wait! There *IS* a new baby! Look at that!	*(Tiptoe slowly forward.)*
Oh! Isn't he tiny! Isn't he cute!	*(Stop—smile—look down—pause.)*
You *ARE* the Christ child!	*(Hold out both bands.)*
This is really the Savior—the Messiah that God promised.	*(Look at one another; nod affirmatively.)*
Come! Let's tell the others what we have found!	*(Run in place.)*
Come! Let's tell them it's the Savior, the Messiah.	*(Continue to run.)*
We found the baby! We found the Christ child!	*(Put hands around mouth as if shouting.)*

Leon Kofod

CELEBRATIONS

MY CHURCH'S BIRTHDAY PARTY

by Stephen D. Jones

GOAL: To feel proud of our church's heritage and where it places us today as we face the future.

INTRODUCTION

In using this intergenerational design, you are probably celebrating a church anniversary, a founder's day, or Pentecost. These are natural times for a church to have a birthday party. But so also might be the beginning of fall when a new program year begins, or even Advent, which is the beginning of the church's liturgical year. In short, you can make up most any excuse to celebrate your church's existence!

Does your church have a heritage? Surely it does, unless it was born yesterday! What are your resources in exploring your heritage? Is there a written history booklet? An old-timer who's collected a scrapbook of church historical items? A box full of old records, old newsletters, etc., in a closet at church? Through various sources, you should be able to find many handles on your church's heritage.

This design may take some homework on your part, depending upon how many resources you have and how available they are. Because each church will need to approach its heritage differently, what follow are various ideas which you can organize to suit your needs. The preparation requirements are therefore listed within each activity.

The important thing is: let people know some interesting things about their heritage, and let it become "their story"! If we can stand together and be proud of this heritage, perhaps we can more courageously face our future as Christ's body in the world.

OPENING THE GATHERING: THE CHURCH'S FAMILY TREE

The people gathered for this party are all members of your church now. But what other churches have been a part of their lives before this one? It might be very interesting to find out how many other churches people have belonged to before they joined this church.

Sometimes when this is done, people discover that they were members of another church in another city about the same time as someone else in the room! Anyway, discovering and recording this information could be an appropriate thing to do as people arrive. Here's how it can be done:

• Cover an entire wall with newsprint. On it write your church's name across the top. Provide pencils or fine-print pens for people to add their information to the Church's Family Tree. Draw a long vertical line from top to bottom in the middle of the newsprint. At the top, write the founding date of your church. Mark off five- or ten-year sections on the line, until you get to the current date at the bottom of the newsprint (see example).

• Families then can draw a horizontal line on the date they joined this church. They should draw their line out until they come to a clear place in the paper, where their line can turn and they can note the churches in their immediate family's history, much like a family tree would look. Dates, places, and the name of the family should be included.

• At some point in the programs, someone could announce the number of church relationships that are represented in your current church membership and other interesting facts gleaned from the newsprint.

• Preparation for the church's family tree must include taping up the newsprint and preparing it. You'll need pencils or pens. Someone will need to stand beside the newsprint to interpret this to families as they arrive. Remember, families can be as few as one person and as many as ____?____!!

DEVELOPING THE EXPERIENCE
History hats

• Ask persons at each table to represent a different period of the church's history. From a booklet or material you pull together, have them browse and decide what was the headline from their period of the church's history. For example, table one has from

EXAMPLE of the CHURCH'S FAMILY TREE

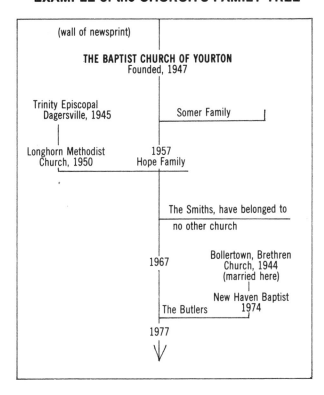

1920–1930. As they ponder the material, they decide that beginning the construction on your current building was the headline from this period.

• After each group has a headline, they can create "history hats" by stapling together folded newspapers. With a marker, write on the face of the newspaper their headline, i.e., WE BUILT OUR BUILDING!, and wear the hats! Hats can be any weird or normal size shape or design! Ask the tables to share their findings. Supplies needed are: staplers and staples, old newspapers, scissors, markers, and historical materials.

An old-timers' dialogue

• Ask two old-timers to dialogue about their memories, with a moderator who can keep things moving along or
• Ask two representatives (previously selected) to dialogue about the decade in which they joined the church or
• Select a well-loved and well-versed old-timer to answer questions which the children and youth have about the history of the church.

Recognize some "record-setters"

• Recognition, even a token prize, can be given to that person who has belonged the longest time or the shortest time, or to all those members who have belonged to no other church, or to people married in the church, or baptized in the church, to the family with the most baptisms, or the most marriages.

Symbolize your heritage

• With children before the party, make up sugar cookie dough. Share several excerpts from the church's history and invite the children to form symbols in the cookie dough. For example, thirty years ago, the church had a pastor who held a community candlelight service on New Year's Eve that attracted hundreds to your church. The custom since has died out, but it was one of the highlights of that period which some people still talk about. The children could roll out the sugar cookie dough, cut out the shape of candles, bake them, and then decorate with icing. The cookies become refreshments for the party as well as a good way to encourage children to explore and communicate their heritage.

Period focus

• Ask a church group (perhaps the youth) to do some research on the times and culture in your community when your church was founded. Information about dress styles, popular music, games, and activities from that period can be secured from older people in your church or community, or from a nearby historical society. A part of the program could feature the music, a fashion show, slides or pictures you have secured of the community, games, and activities the people enjoyed. Your local library might also be a resource here.

An artist's contribution

• Commission a poem, a song, a skit, a sketching, or a banner that captures a sense of your heritage to be created by a member of your congregation. Nearly every congregation has someone with a special talent, and it needn't even be a well-known talent. Discover somebody! If you "commission" someone to do something to be unveiled at the church's birthday party, he or she just might put himself or herself into it.

A quiz

• Have a true-false quiz about the church's history. Team people for the quiz, putting old-timers and newcomers together, children with adults, grandparents with youth. Try to include some humorous incidents and even some silly questions with simple answers, for example, what denomination was this church when it was formed? How long have you been a member? Did this church sing hymns when it first began?

• Combine teams into groups of six or eight to compare answers.

• Conclude with general sharing, answering any questions that stumped the entire group.

Songs to sing

• "The Church's One Foundation"
• "I Love Thy Kingdom, Lord"
• "God of our Fathers"
• "Sons of God"
• "The Church Within Us"
• "Lord, I Want to Be a Christian"

CLOSING THE GATHERING

To close, affirm your church and/or express hopes for your church.

• To do this, you'll need to cut out of a large sheet of butcher paper *two* identical copies of a *large* human body, as appears below:

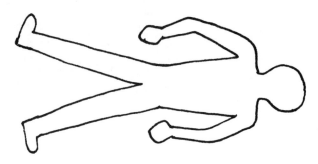

Cut one copy of the body into as many pieces as you will have participants in your program. A few extra pieces won't hurt, as they can be seen as affirmations and hopes of future members.

Place these pieces over the other uncut copy of the body, tracing out each piece on it. Number each piece

and its corresponding place on the uncut copy as follows:

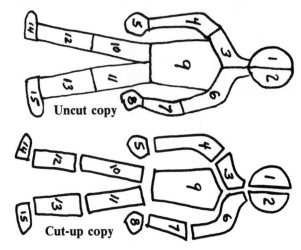

Uncut copy

Cut-up copy

• When the time for closing comes, read 1 Corinthians 12:12-27 and point out that here the church is described as a body.

• Gather in a circle around the paper body which is lying on the floor with the cut pieces in place on top of the uncut copy. Ask each person to pick up one cut piece of the body, and on that write one or two words affirming what this church has meant to him or her or expressing a hope of what it can be in the future. (Be sure to have pens available.)

• When all are ready, ask them one by one to place their numbered pieces back on top of the body in the appropriate places, sharing their affirmation or hope.

• Close with a prayer and a song, holding hands as you encircle this symbolic body.

• Afterward, you might tape the loose pieces onto the uncut copy and carry this paper body up to the front lobby area of your church and leave it on the floor. People can walk over it, read it, and think about it on the next Sunday.

Stephen D. Jones is on the staff of the First Baptist Church of Dayton, Ohio.

BIRTHDAY—LAUNCH DAY

by Stephen D. Jones

GOAL: To think of our birthdays as launch days into 365 days of New Life, and to rehearse and plan for our coming birthdays in our families.

INTRODUCTION

In this design people are encouraged to take a new and different approach to celebrating birthdays in their families or with their closest friends. A leader who can help people feel comfortable using their imaginations is needed for the experience. The steps for leading this program are written in the form of a script for the leader. It is *not* intended that the script be used word for word. But rather, it is a resource from which the leader can glean ideas for his or her own unique approach.

Treat this experience as a rehearsal for families and friends! The chances of someone having a birthday on the day of your event are not great; so nearly everyone will be rehearsing for a future day, but that's the key ingredient in the enjoyment of the event! The leader's responsibility will be to help people have fun with their imaginations!

PREPARATION
You will need:

1. One hour and one-half, but feel free to adapt the suggestions to the time you have available.
2. For the Birthday Armbands: construction paper, scissors, tape, markers.
3. For Birthday Planning: print envelopes that have the directions on the outside, also sheets of paper mimeographed with the appropriate questionnaire.
4. For the Hope Cards: slips of paper and pencils, white poster board for each family, markers, pieces of wrapped candy, stamp pads, other decorative materials, tape, glue.
5. Overhead or opaque projector or chalkboard.
6. For the Symbolic Gifts: pipe cleaners.
7. For the Launch Day Passage: on the back of the planning questionnaire, print the Ephesians 1 paraphrase.

8. For the Affirmation Prayer: print out the opening and closing sentences for all to read.
9. For a song and a cake: have cupcakes, candles, and matches available. Print out the words of the song for all to see.

TIMING AND PROCEDURE
Opening the gathering (3 minutes)

"Most of us never think of planning the celebration of our own birthdays. In our society, that's the responsibility of those who love us—our families and closest friends. They are the ones who bake the cakes, purchase the gifts, invite the guests. And, more often than not, when we celebrate our birthdays, we do so with one eye looking back over our shoulder, thinking of the year we have just completed. With a sigh of relief we might say, 'Well, I finally made it. Another year gone by.' We look *back* on birthdays.

"What if your next birthday was to be different? What if your next birthday celebration was one that you planned? What if the major decisions of who, what, and how many were yours? And what if, on your next birthday, instead of looking back over the past year, you looked *forward* to your coming year?

"What if you understood your next birthday as your LAUNCH DAY INTO 365 DAYS OF NEW LIFE!?! Can you see these coming days, weeks, and months as God's gift to you?

"So your next birthday celebration is to be one that launches you in the right direction and with the right tempo into your coming year. It is to launch you with enthusiasm, with hope, with eagerness.

"In this event you'll be answering this question: "What will it take for me to launch into 365 days of New Life?"

Developing the experience (see time markings by each activity)

1. "This experience will be a rehearsal for the birthdays you will celebrate with your family and/or closest friends in the coming year. We'll be

doing several activities here that you can take into your homes and repeat on your birthdays."

2. *Birthday Armbands* (15 minutes)

"First, let's do something around our birthdays. You've all seen armbands that become a symbol of power and pride. Armbands have been used by militant blacks, or by the Women's Movement, by the Gray Panthers, and by many others. So, we want you to be proud of your birthday month, and be proud of what it means. We'll ask all those whose birthday is in January to go to the *southwest corner* of the room. Those with February birthdays will please go _____." Assign each month to a different part of the same room and ask persons whose birthday is in that month to go to that area. After everyone has arrived in the appropriate place, give these directions.

• "Now will each month come up with an armband that each of you can create and then wear? You have construction paper, scissors, tape, and markers. With these you can make an appropriate armband that displays the pride you have in your month. I'll give you only six minutes to create these."

• After six minutes, having given several time warnings, ask the group for each month to show its armbands to the total group.

3. *Getting in Family Groups* (4 minutes)

• "For the rest of this program you'll need to be in family groups. For those who are here with three or more family members, please find a place to sit together. For those who are here tonight in a family group of one or two, we'll ask you to join another family and create an 'extended family' of four to six members. Get together with others whom you know well. Now, please join your family groups."

4. *Handing Out Birthday Planning Materials* (5 minutes)

• "We're handing out envelopes now which say, 'Enclosed are our birthday plans for our family members.' "

John	,	Jan. 5,
(Name)		(next birthday)
_____	,	_____
_____	,	_____
_____	,	_____
_____	,	_____
_____	,	_____

• "Each family unit can take one of these. Later, at the end of the session, each of us will fill in a questionnaire regarding plans for our next birthday. We'll pass it out now." (The questionnaire should look like this.):

NAME: _____

NEXT BIRTHDAY: _____

A Birthday Statement: (State what you'd like to have happen at your next birthday that will launch your coming 365 days of New Life.) _____

_____

Who's to be invited: _____

Other specifics: When? Where? Entertainment? Food? _____

---

5. *Hope Cards* (32 minutes)

• "But first, we're going to do several activities that will help us think about a birthday launch day. Birthday cards are a part of nearly everyone's day. So, select one family member whose birthday is the furthest away from today, and create a birthday card for that person. And since this birthday is to be a launch day, there's nothing better to launch a person off into the new year than telling her or him what hopes you have for her or him. You need to relate to the person what potential and possibility you see for that person in the coming 365 days.

• "With the slips of paper you'll find on each table, each family member will write down two specific hopes you have for the member on whose birthday you're focusing. If today really were this person's birthday, what specific hopes would you have for him or her in the coming year? BE HONEST! For example, you might hope for this person an improved golf score, greater strength to cope with difficulties at work, a chance finally to complete painting the outside of the house, or having many occasions to express love for an oldest daughter.

• "Each of you write your specific hopes for this person now. Write at least ten hopes all together for this person. (Provide five minutes to do this.)

• "Now, hand all of your notes to the family members for whom you've hoped, and let's have those persons select the eight that they feel will launch them most effectively into their next year.

• "After the eight hopes have been selected, a

family member can come up to the head table and pick up a large white sheet of poster board, markers, wrapped candy, a stamp pad, and other decorative materials. On this poster board, you'll be creating a birthday card that expresses your hope.

• "If you'll look on the overhead projector (or opaque projector, or chalkboard), you'll see an example. On the outer fringes of this card are the hopes that Frank's family has for him, which he selected. On the inside are the signature and thumb-print of each family member, and a simple message.

• "Make your hope cards, and give them to the intended person. You'll have twenty minutes to do this."

EXAMPLE OF THE HOPE CARD

6. *Symbolic Gifts* (7 minutes)
   • "Every birthday we also give gifts. For these same family members, create a symbolic gift out of pipe

cleaners that will help them as they live out their hoped-for year.

• "For example, if I hoped that Frank's golf game would improve, a pipe cleaner bent into the shape of a golf club would help. If I hoped that Frank's worries at the office would minimize, I might bend the cleaner into a wrinkle on one end and keep it smooth on the other. If I hoped that Frank would have more times to talk with his daughter, I might shape two hands close together. So, let's have a time for making the gifts, and then present them to the family members."

7. *Launch Day Passage* (4 minutes)
   "Now let's pick on another family member for a while! Select the family member whose birthday is the closest to today. You're going to read, in unison, a passage of Scripture from the Bible. We'll call it a 'Launch Day Passage.' When you actually celebrate the real birthdays in your home, you might like to look in the Bible beforehand, select an appropriate passage, and paraphrase it to fit as a Launch Day Passage. But for this experience, we'll read Ephesians 1 which has already been rewritten for you. You'll find it on the back of the questionnaire previously distributed. And as we read in unison, adding those family members and names whose birthdays are the nearest to today, let's have those honored family members stand.

• "PRAISE BE TO GOD, _____,
                                    (family member's name)
who has so freely given you every needed thing for your spiritual happiness.

_____, God chose you before
       (name)
you were born, and dedicated himself to see that your life is filled with love. God gave you your future destiny, _____,
                                              (name)
and you are fully accepted as his (son) (daughter). In Christ, you will be liberated from that which imprisons; your stumbling-blocks can be removed.
Your sins and your guilt, God will completely for-
    give.
God has been lavish, giving you wisdom and in-
    sight.
And God calls you to have hope.
When you hear these promises, believe in them, for they are the Best News available for your life!!"

---

8. *Affirmation Prayer* (9 minutes)

"Now pick another family member for our next part of any Launch Day Birthday! To launch off into the future, you must feel affirmed, you must feel good about yourself. To affirm means to tell someone what it is you really appreciate in them. Tell them what you like about them. Begin the prayer with these words,

'God, hear us as we affirm,

_____.'
(name)

And then, go around the circle of your family and say affirmative things about this person. Try to focus on some things that person might not realize about himself or herself.

- "Close the prayer by each saying,
'God, we thank you for _____
(name)
and for life! Amen!'"

9. *A Song and a Cake* (10 minutes)

- "Do you have another family member who's not been sitting in the Birthday Hot Seat? It's time for them now! If you've run out of family members, go back to the first member who was considered this evening. We're going to sing a song familiar to birthdays, 'Happy Birthday to You.'
We'll sing a new verse, and then an old verse,

'We thank God for life,
We thank God for love,
We thank God for everyone,
But mostly for you.

'Happy Birthday to you,
Happy Launch Day to you,
Happy Birthday, dear _____,
(name)
Happy Launch Day to you!'

- "But we've go to have candles and cake, right? Out from the kitchen come cupcakes for everyone, and, you guessed it, a candle for everyone with a book of matches for each family member. If one family member will get a cupcake for each member of your family as the cart goes around, we'll give you the signal to light your candles, and sing together. . . ."

Closing the gathering (10 minutes)

"In conclusion, take out the questionnaire about your birthday, and fill it in. Perhaps you'd like to make sure some things from this evening's program happen on your real birthday. Put your requests, unknown to the rest of your family, in your family envelope. Just before each person's birthday, the family can open the envelope and plan for the upcoming Birthday-Launch Day. And I hope you'll be having many happy birthdays in the coming year! Happy birthday, everyone!!!"

Stephen D. Jones is on the staff of the First Baptist Church of Dayton, Ohio.

USING MEDIA WITH THE CHURCH FAMILY

by Ed Heuer

Have you ever had the experience of watching an ordinary television program and gradually becoming aware that there appears to be a message coming through the story—a point, a moral, or whatever?

To go a step further, have you ever had the vague notion that you were receiving a *biblical* message from such a story? "Star Trek," "The Waltons," "Little House on the Prairie," "Welcome Back, Kotter," and even "All in the Family" have provided that kind of experience for some. But when we do receive such a message, we seldom follow through on our vague notion with a little thought, discussion, and research.

FORMS OF MEDIA

The next three programs illustrate ways in which contemporary media can be used as a resource for enriching our present understandings of the biblical message and enhancing the development of our faith.

Television

Television, often viewed as the "curse of our age," offers one of the richest sources for learning, primarily because it is so available to the family. By stopping to discuss an interesting program, rather than simply sitting to view one program after another, the family can create an opportunity to share values, insights, and faith. Intergenerational groups within the church provide a similar opportunity.

When attempting to use television in church groups, the planner/leader faces two problems: (1) securing advance knowledge of program content, and (2) matching a convenient group meeting time with the scheduled broadcast time.

Several publications, some free, are available which provide a guide to programs considered especially worthwhile (see the resource list). Some guides will also provide a synopsis of content and suggestions for study. Such publications are quite helpful in solving the first problem.

The problem of matching viewing time with group meeting time is more difficult to solve. Even though new technology and declining prices are making videotape recorders more affordable, this equipment is still beyond the budget of most local churches. However, many churches include a member with access to such equipment for occasional use. Groups of churches have also been known to purchase videotape recorders on a cooperative basis. If your community is served by cable television, check with the operator of the cable television franchise. He can often provide facilities both to preview a program and cablecast it at a time convenient for viewing by groups.

Families should be aware of the impact of television in their homes. It can be used for moral and even religious education. The time is coming when it will be more accessible to local churches as well on a larger scale.

Films

Film, drama, puppets, and music can provide highly effective shared experiences for a church group. Each offers unique benefits. Film, for instance, offers a wide choice of subjects, in formats ranging from a few minutes to several hours. Film can be readily previewed or shown a second time to allow a group to pursue deeper levels of meaning which are seldom perceived in a single viewing.

Drama

Drama, puppets, and music may be used effectively for the purpose of presenting a subject, but each of these also offers a special chance for direct participation in the medium itself. Such participation can further enrich a learning experience.

LEARNING FROM MEDIA

It is important to remember that without proper reflection on a media experience most of its learning value will be lost. Intergenerational group reflection on a shared media experience offers a rich opportunity for learning, as each person can hear both "the voice of experience" and the precocious insights that come "out of the mouths of babes," and at the same time experience the moving of the Holy Spirit among the fellowship.

It is a gift; open it, and use it!

RESOURCE LIST
Films

Recommended Films (check with distributor or your denominational film library for current rental prices):

1. *A Fuzzy Tale,* Mass Media Ministries, 2116 N. Charles Street, Baltimore, MD 21218.
2. *Oh Happy Day,* same distributor.
3. *William,* TeleKETICS, 1229 So. Santee St., Los Angeles, CA 90015.
4. *Hello Up There,* Learning Corporation of America, 711 Fifth Ave., New York, NY 10022.

Recommended Periodicals Providing Film Reviews:

1. *Mass Media Newsletter* (twice monthly) from Mass Media Ministries, 2116 N. Charles St., Baltimore, MD 21218. $12 per year.
2. *Media Mix* (eight times per year) from Claretian Publications, 221 W. Madison St., Chicago, IL 60606. $9 per year.

Television

Recommended Periodicals Offering Advance Reviews of Television Programs Recommended for Religious or Educational Use:

1. *Teacher's Guide to Television* P.O. Box 564, Lenox Hill Station, New York, NY 10021. $4 for two semesters.
2. *Mass Media Newsletter* (see *Films*)

Drama

Recommended Sources for Plays and Dramatic Resources:

1. The Sharing Company; P.O. Box 2224, Austin, TX 78767. Write for their free listing of short plays and worship ideas.
2. Contemporary Drama Service; Box 457, 1131 Warren Ave., Downers Grove, IL 60515. Write for their free catalog of "hard-to-find participation resources."
3. Plays for Living; Family Service Association of America, 44 East 23rd Street, New York, NY 10010.

Ed Heuer is Minister of Education in the First Baptist Church of Hyattsville, Maryland.

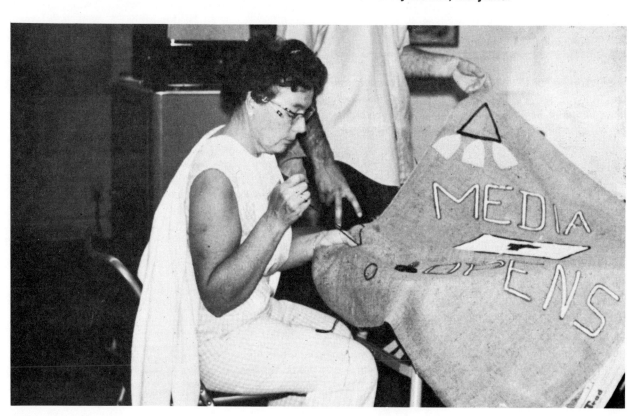

THE GRICKLE-GRASS PROPHET

by Ed Heuer

GOAL: To reflect on a television program and explore biblical materials related to it. To see how television programs can be used in the church.

INTRODUCTION

The television program which has been chosen for this experience offers a wide range of opportunities for enrichment of some of our own biblical understandings. *The Lorax* (based on the book of the same name by Dr. Seuss) is still sometimes aired in the spring or early summer as a children's special. Major biblical themes, such as justice, idolatry, and stewardship of the creation, are apparent in the story.

The Lorax is also available in 16mm film format, making the content of this TV program available for preview. Libraries have the book, and the film is available for free loan through many public library film collections.

The leader of the session should preview the story in some form, making notes on any biblical themes the story suggests to him or her. Then, locate a relevant passage and study it prayerfully, looking for further parallels between the biblical passage and the story. Chapters 4 and 5 of Amos offer an additional biblical perspective that should be considered by the leader in preparation for this session. Such "digging" produces new insights as the Holy Spirit enables a creative synthesis of a timely story and the timeless Word. The study process will work even better in a planning group where the joy of sharing is an added gift.

A word on the medium of television: For many reasons it is unlikely that a church program can be scheduled to coincide with an actual broadcast of *The Lorax*. Communities with cable TV or churches with access to videotape recording equipment will have a better chance to use TV programs at convenient times as a regular part of their church family programs. Though *The Lorax* was chosen to be presented by television, it can be shown as a 16 mm film, or even read from the book in small groups.

PREPARATION
You will need:

1. An hour and fifteen minutes
2. A room suited for television viewing in groups of twenty people per TV set, having sufficient space for limited moving about
3. Copies of the Bible in a variety of translations (participants should be asked to bring their personal study Bibles, but extra copies will be necessary for those who forget)
4. Copies of concordances, Bible dictionaries, and commentaries (at least one of each for every ten people expected to attend)
5. Paper and pencils, newsprint and marking pen
6. Brightly colored construction paper and markers for making name tags, as well as pins or tape for attaching them
7. Brightly colored construction paper and poster-board for the construction of decorations, scissors, masking tape
8. One television set (19" diagonal screen or larger) for every twenty people expected
9. A table or stand at least three feet high for each television set
10. A copy of the book *The Lorax* (optional)
11. One package of sunflower seeds to plant
12. One person to lead the session
13. One person to set up and attend to the TV sets (or VTR equipment, or 16mm projector if these are used)

Things to do ahead of time

1. Preview the story as indicated in the "Introduction" above.
2. Arrange the room for convenient TV viewing in groups of not more than twenty per set.
3. Decorate the room with a forest of Truffula trees (made from construction paper, see the book for a picture of a Truffula tree). Make one large Truffula tree with a *trunk* at least five feet tall, to be used as part of the evaluation portion of the program.

4. Set up a table for making name tags, and make a set of instructions on newsprint to be posted nearby. Suggest that each person use the construction paper to make a Dr. Seuss-type caricature of himself or herself as a name tag. Tearing the name tags out of the construction paper will help to give them that authentic Dr. Seuss look.
5. Arrange for pencils, paper, Bibles, and the reference books to be placed conveniently for handing out later.
6. The sunflower seeds are for a surprise at the end. Have them handy, but hidden.
7. Ask your co-worker to arrive early to help set up and check out the equipment.

Publicity

1. Contact the local TV station to see if you can get a ten-second public service announcement about your program, preferably just after one of the advance promotional spot announcements of the upcoming children's television special, "The Lorax."
2. Construction paper Truffula trees would make good posters. There is a lot of room for information on the roundish foliage at the top of the tree. Be certain that the posters remind each person to bring a Bible to the session.

PROCEDURE AND TIMING
Opening the gathering (15 minutes)

1. Greet the people as they arrive, and direct them to the name-tag table.
2. Five minutes before the program is to be aired, ask people to find a seat, dividing the group so that approximately the same number of people will be watching each set. You may want to turn on each TV set to help get their attention, but leave the sound off as you give them instructions for watching the program.

Developing the experience (50 minutes)

1. Ask a few people to pass out pencils and paper. Explain that some people who have watched "The Lorax" in the past have been reminded by it of things they have read or heard about in the Bible or at church. Suggest that if some of this group have a similar experience while watching the show, they should make a note of it on their paper (in the case of children too small to write, they may want to draw a picture of part of the program). Although not all people will find something to write about (which is all right), urge everyone to try, even if they are able to remember only part of what they have heard or read. Suggest that during the commercials people might share their thoughts; this will help to put others on the track.
2. Watch the program together.
3. Immediately following the program, ask the group to remain seated so participants can be divided into subgroups. These should be made up of eight to ten people of all ages (no all-children, all-youth, or all-adult groups).

   • First ask those who have recorded something on their paper to stand. If there are relatively few, ask them to move to different parts of the room so they can serve as the gathering points for forming subgroups.

   • Ask others to move to one of these gathering points, trying to form groups of equal size and mixed ages.

   • If there are many who stand, quickly select a few as gathering points and suggest that a group should not be made up entirely of people who have notes or of those who have none.

4. Once the groups have been formed, each person who has recorded something should share it with the group. After all have shared, it will be the task of the group to select one or two biblical passages that seem to be most relevant (do this quickly).

   • Each group should then begin a study of the passage to determine its context and meaning. The leader can be passing out the reference books (concordances, etc.) as people are sharing their notes, so the reference books will be available in each group to help them locate and study the passages they have chosen.

   • If a group appears to be stuck, the leader can suggest a passage or two from his or her study in preparation for the session.

5. When there are about ten minutes left in the hour, suggest that each group use the remaining time to discuss how well the passage and the story of the The Lorax fit together.

   • Ask: "Is there anything about the story of The Lorax that helps you to better understand the passage?"

   • "Is there anything about the passage that helps to explain some of the things that happened in the story?"

6. Just before their time is up, ask each group to

appoint a reporter to share with the larger group. Each reporter should try to:

(1) Give the references and a brief description of the passages studied.

(2) Briefly share any insights as to how the Scripture and program were related.

Evaluating and closing the gathering (15 minutes)

1. Ask everyone to gather his or her chair into the circle for a closing summary.

2. Ask the representative of each group to report. Record the different passages on newsprint or a chalkboard.

3. Explain that you'd like each person to help evaluate the program for the evening *after the benediction,* but that you want to give instructions for the evaluation now.

 • Ask each person to (1) write any comments he or she has on the back of his or her name tag; then (2), before going home, pin all the name tags on the trunk of the large Truffula tree.

 • Ask them to evaluate the evening's activity on the basis of learning something new either from the Bible itself or about the way that media and the Bible can shed light on each other. If the learning was truly worthwhile to participants, ask them to pin their name tags at or near the top of the *trunk* of the tree. If they experienced no learning value, ask them to pin the name tags at the bottom. Those who feel that the value of the learning was somewhere between the two extremes should put their name tags on the appropriate part of the trunk of the Truffula tree.

4. Ask group members to stand in a circle for the benediction; and as they do so, pass out a sunflower seed to each one. Return to your place and announce that the benediction for the evening will be a reading from the last page of the book *The Lorax* and from the prophecy of Amos (9:13-15, *The Living Bible*). Add "Amen" or "So be it" at the end.

Ed Heuer is Minister of Education at the First Baptist Church of Hyattsville, Maryland.

USING TELEVISION, FILMS, AND DRAMA

DISCIPLES: THE WARM, FUZZY PEOPLE

by Ed Heuer

GOALS: To identify ways of demonstrating discipleship through acts of love. To see how film can be used with all ages in church programs.

INTRODUCTION

This session is designed to help participants create a synthesis of Scripture and film. The text is John 13:34-35. The film is *A Fuzzy Tale.* The passage offers a perspective from which group members can view the film and provides a basis by which they can respond to it. The central concept is discipleship, showing that acts of love are basic to identifying oneself as a disciple of Jesus Christ.

Rented films usually arrive at least three days early, and an early previewing of the film will allow the leader adequate time to reflect on its relationship to the text. It is important to achieve a synthesis of the Scripture and the film if the leader is to serve as an enabler for the church family group.

PREPARATION
You will need:

1. An hour and fifteen minutes
2. A room large enough for your group to move freely, with chairs for some if the floor is carpeted and for all if it is not
3. Copies of the Bible, preferably RSV
4. The film *A Fuzzy Tale* (Order from: Mass Media Ministries, 2116 N. Charles St., Baltimore, MD 21218. Rent $18)
5. A 16mm sound projector with take-up reel and a projection screen
6. Materials for name tags: construction paper in warm colors (yellow, orange, etc.), pins, and marking pens
7. "Fuzzy" materials: one skein of yarn and a pair of scissors for every six people in your group; yarn should be of warm colors, preferably variegated
8. Several helpers in addition to the session leader; a projectionist and one assistant for every eighteen people in the total group
9. A record player and LP record for background music at the beginning and during group working sessions. Try to find an LP record that reinforces the theme, such as a children's record.

Things to do ahead of time

1. Arrange the room for viewing the film. Set up chairs, make provision to darken the room, and prepare the projector and screen (try to set up so the picture will fill the screen entirely).
2. Cut construction paper into 4" x 6" name tags, and set up a place where people can make their own name tags as they arrive.
3. Cut the skein of yarn into 25' lengths for each participant you anticipate coming.
4. Prepare copies of the discussion questions for each group of six people.
5. Set up the record player in an out-of-the-way area.
6. Each assistant will act as a helper with three subgroups of six people. Ask helpers to arrive a few minutes early so you can explain their responsibility to them.

Publicity

1. Posters around the church and announcements in the church bulletin or newsletter will usually do the job; but be certain to use the title of the program to generate curiosity. If a church family gathering is new to your church, a special invitation mailed to each family of your church will help to promote interest.
2. Nothing beats plain, old "talkin' it up!"

PROCEDURE AND TIMING
Opening the gathering (10 minutes):

1. Turn on the record player about ten minutes before people are to arrive; set the volume low enough so they can talk.

2. Greet people as they arrive and ask each to make a name tag. Encourage mingling.

3. About ten minutes after starting time ask everyone to find a seat facing the screen.

Developing the experience (50 minutes)

1. Introduce the program and the film with a mini-speech (under five minutes), covering the following points:

   a. Title of the program: "Disciples: The Warm, Fuzzy People."

   b. Title of the film, *A Fuzzy Tale.*

   c. Discipleship: Jesus called all of us to be disciples, but *being* a disciple isn't always easy. (To involve the children present, you might ask: "What do disciples do?")

   d. Read the text, John 13:34-35, using the Revised Standard Version. Emphasize "have love" in verse 35.

   e. If Jesus came today to explain discipleship, he might have used a film instead of parables.

2. Show the film *A Fuzzy Tale* (12 minutes).

3. After the film, ask people to gather in non-family mixed-age groups of five or six (small children may remain with parents). Do not have any all-adult, all-children or all-youth groups. Assistants then pass out the skein of yarn, scissors, Bible, and the discussion questions to each group as it forms.

4. Explain that for the next half hour each group is to make "Warm Fuzzies" using the yarn, and that they are to discuss five questions as they work on the fuzzies.

   a. Instructions for fuzzies: take a 25-foot length of yarn and wrap it around one hand until 8 inches are left. Cut off the 8-inch piece, and use it to tie the wrapped piece in the middle (like a figure 8). Cut all the loops at each end and roll the ball of yarn between your hand like clay. Voila! A Warm Fuzzy! Suggest experimentation to make other kinds of symbolic fuzzies, as time allows. Your assistants can help any having trouble.

   b. Discussion questions (suggest each group spend about 5 minutes on each question except #4).

      (1) If being a disciple means showing love (giving fuzzies), how many ways can your group recall that love was shown in the movie?

      (2) Were there any people in the movie who acted like Jesus? Who? How?

      (3) Which kind of people *needed* to be shown love in the movie?

      (4) Who needs to be shown love in our own church and community? (Allow 10 minutes for this question.)

      (5) Have each person in your group tell one way in which he or she will show love to another person by tomorrow.

5. After the discussion, ask each person to give a fuzzy to another "to keep."

Evaluating and closing the gathering (10 minutes)

1. To evaluate, ask people how they feel about the program. Have them respond by placing themselves along an imaginary continuum (use an open wall).

   • Those who feel like the program was a warm fuzzy should go to one end of the room. Those who feel like it was a cold prickly should go to the other end. Those who feel somewhere in between should locate at the appropriate spot between the extremes. Ask if anyone wants to comment.

   • If there are people near the cold prickly end, *solicit* their comments to reconcile them with the group.

2. Ask everyone to bless the whole group with a singing benediction. Join in a circle and sing "They'll Know We are Christians by Our Love."

Ed Heuer is Minister of Education in the First Baptist Church of Hyattsville, Maryland.

USING TELEVISION, FILMS, AND DRAMA

NOW, IF THAT HAD BEEN ME . . .

by Ed Heuer

GOAL: To involve each person in a dramatic reenactment of the "original temptation" in order to reflect on what it means to be tempted and what it means to be a responsible person.

INTRODUCTION

This session is designed to allow all of the participants to share in a media experience. The medium is drama, and the biblical resources are drawn from Genesis 3:1-7. The open-ended playlet used in this session takes a degree of poetic license with the passage in the interest of focusing attention on one of several themes developed by the text. The theme under consideration here is personal responsibility for one's own decision.

PREPARATION
You will need:

1. An hour and fifteen minutes.
2. A space large enough to create a theater-in-the-round with a stage area at least twelve feet in diameter and additional room for the required number of chairs to accommodate your group.
3. Tables, enough to allow each person a small work area for coloring and gluing
4. A few Bibles for reference
5. Copies of the playlet, "Meanwhile, Back in the Garden," for each member of the cast (4)
6. One copy of each of the puppet faces for each participant; see the samples at the end of this program
7. Glue sticks, crayons, and scissors for use by everyone
8. Lunch bags for every person in the group
9. A record player and the LP record: Flip Wilson: "The Devil Made Me Buy This Dress," Little David Records (Stereo/LD-1000)
10. A leader to direct the experience and an assistant if the group is larger than thirty
11. Cast of four for the playlet (Memorization of lines

and a few rehearsals will enhance the experience for the audience, but the play can be read if necessary. However, at *least* two advance readings are necessary so that the characters can distinguish the dialogue from the stage directions and achieve some feel for the content.)

Things to do ahead of time

1. Set up the room, placing tables around the outer edge and making a large circle of chairs to create the stage area.
2. Make a cardboard tree at least five feet tall (finished on both sides) and place it in the center of the stage area. Hang fruit on the tree (see stage directions in the script for details).
3. Ask the cast to arrive at least a half hour early for a final rehearsal.
4. Arrange a place for making name tags; have pins or tape for attaching them. Make a sign giving directions for making name tags: Each person selects one of the four puppet faces to use as a name tag; cuts it out and decorates it as the person wishes.
5. Gather other materials (i.e., crayons, glue, scissors, additional puppet faces, and lunch bags).
6. Set up a record player and have the Flip Wilson record set up to be played later (Side A, track 2).
7. Brief the cast of the playlet and your assistant about the timing of their parts of the program.

Publicity

1. A poster containing all the vital information about the program is a good idea. Make an apple out of construction paper and attach it to the poster with Scotch Tape at the top, like a hinge. On the apple write, "DO NOT LOOK UNDER THIS APPLE."
On the part of the poster covered by the apple, write: "You're no better than Adam and Eve" in small letters. Above the apple, write: "Now if that had been you in the Garden of Eden. . . ."
2. If you have a committee to help you, canvass the

church membership by phone. Sometimes a personal invitation will bring people out.

3. This is a good program to share with people outside the church; it will let them know that church people experience temptation, too. Try handbilling the neighborhood for three blocks in each direction around the church. You'll need at least six hundred handbills and a dozen workers to do it in about a half hour.

PROCEDURE AND TIMING
Opening the gathering (15 minutes)

1. Greet people as they arrive, and direct each to make a name tag.
2. About five minutes after the starting time, ask everyone to find a seat, and start the Flip Wilson record.
3. With the record as a light introduction to the topic, go on to explain that the group will be sharing some experiences related to temptation. The purpose is to help everyone understand our responsibility for the decisions we make when we are tempted. Explain that a play based on the temptation of Adam and Eve will be presented next. Let people know that the play will be brief (5 to 8 minutes) and that it will be loosely based on the third chapter of Genesis.

Developing the experience (50 minutes)

1. Present the playlet.
2. Ask for immediate reactions to the play. The point that each of us has a responsibility for his or her own decisions is fairly obvious. Let the comments and discussion in the group go on just long enough to have the group affirm the point—preferably by several age levels.
3. Explain that you want to divide them into groups. Ask all the children from kindergarten to sixth grade to get together in groups of three. Then ask for adult volunteers who like to work with children, and assign one to each group of three children. Do the same with junior highs, and repeat again with senior highs. Finally, ask all the remaining adults to get together in groups of four (suggest a mixing of church people and visitors). Now you should have everyone assigned to a group of four.
4. Explain that each group will have twenty minutes to make four hand puppets from the lunch bags and the puppet faces.
   - Each of the groups is to share the kinds of

temptations that they have to face, and then decide on one kind of temptation to illustrate in a short puppet play.
   - Construct puppets to suit the characters needed for the puppet play.
   - The idea here is to develop a series of puppet plays to illustrate the kinds of temptations experienced at different age levels. The adult in each group of children and youth is there to enable and help the group operate within the time limits.
   - Remind these helpers to encourage input by the children and youth and to avoid speaking for them.
5. When there are about thirty minutes left, announce that it is time to finish up the work on puppets and on the short puppet skit.
   - Have each group present its skit. Invite expressions of appreciation after each performance, but try to keep the pace moving so attention won't lag.
   - If the group is very large, there will not be time for every small group to put on a play for the big group. The leader may need to move through the groups to find one or two small groups from each age level who are most prepared to present a skit with their puppets.
   - Or, the leader can suggest that a children's group, a youth group, and an adult group give their plays for each other. This would mean several groups of a dozen persons giving their plays in different corners of the room.

Closing the gathering (10 minutes)

1. After the last puppet skit, try to draw the experience together (you may want to make notes during the puppet shows). Points to listen for might include: the devil can't make us do anything we don't want to do; to blame the devil for our problems is to "pass the buck"; we believe in the forgiveness of God, and by God's grace we *can* take responsibility for our decisions and meet our temptations with a measure of confidence.
2. Ask everyone to gather in a circle for the closing prayer. When all are quiet, ask them to join together in the Lord's Prayer.
3. Immediately after the "Amen" ask everyone to use a crayon to draw a big smile or frown on his or her name tag as an evaluation of the program. Designate a place for them to drop off their name tags as they leave.

MEANWHILE, BACK IN THE GARDEN

A Playlet in One Act

by Ed Heuer

CAST

NARRATOR (female), provides direction for the sequence of events.

ADAM (male, youth or young adult).

EVE (female, youth or young adult).

TEMPTER (male).

SETTING

No costumes are required for the play. It is to be staged in a miniature theater-in-the-round formed by the chairs of the audience. The circle of chairs should leave an opening at least twelve feet in diameter as the stage area. Additional concentric rows of chairs may be added if the audience is large. There should be two aisles or openings to the stage. A cardboard tree bearing several pieces of fruit should stand at the center of the stage. The fruit is to be in the shape of a question mark cut from cardboard and made sticky (using double-sided carpet tape on the cardboard fruit is ideal). Each piece of fruit should be about six inches long. The question-mark fruit should be stuck on the tree upside-down so as to look like a pear. Six pieces of fruit on the tree will be adequate. The tree should be about five feet tall. A portable lectern will be needed for the NARRATOR.

PLAY

LIGHTS OUT BRIEFLY TO SIGNAL START OF PLAY (*As lights go on, the NARRATOR enters carrying a lectern and walks slowly around the tree, finally stopping next to one of the entrances to the circle.*)

NARRATOR (*slowly, with a sense of awe*): In the beginning, God created the heavens . . . the earth . . . and that attractive couple over there. (*Pause as ADAM and EVE enter from the opposite side holding hands.*) God also created a garden in which Adam and Eve were to live; and in that garden God planted a tree—(*with awe*) a very special tree. The tree was called the tree *of* the fruit *of* the

knowledge *of* good and evil. (*ADAM and EVE move closer to the tree and reach out to touch the fruit.*) DON'T DO THAT!

EVE (*pulling back in surprise*): Why not?

NARRATOR (*relieved that they did not touch the tree*): Just don't do that! God told you that you could eat the fruit from any of the trees except this one; so hands off, OK?

ADAM (*peeved*): God never said we couldn't touch it.

EVE (*a little angry*): God just told us not to eat the fruit; that's all. We hadn't even really given it a thought until *you* started talking about it again. Who made you the boss, anyway?

NARRATOR: I . . . speak for God, and what God meant was STAY AWAY FROM THE TREE. Got that?

EVE (*defiantly starts to reach out to touch a piece of the fruit, but withdraws her hand*): I wasn't really going to touch it anyway. Come on, Adam, let's get something *good* to eat.

(*ADAM and EVE exit the way they entered. NARRATOR shakes her head as she watches them leave, takes a deep breath, and continues.*)

NARRATOR: Now the Tempter was more subtle than any other creature that God had made. (*TEMPTER sneaks up behind the NARRATOR and puts his arm around her waist, puckers his lips, and makes kissing noises directed to the audience. NARRATOR is coolly aloof as she continues.*) Well, maybe subtle isn't quite the right word. (*The TEMPTER recoils in mock surprise, then tiptoes in high-stepping, exaggerated stealth and hides behind the tree.*) The Tempter is, oh, how shall I say it . . . SNEAKY!

Something comes, and you have to make a decision—an important decision. You don't even notice that he's around. Then all of a sudden, just as you are in the middle of making that decision, there he is—filling your head with all kinds of thoughts, and most of them are selfish. He's different from other people though, different from the kind who try to get you into trouble for their benefit. You know, like the kid who tries to get you to steal some candy and then share it with him. He's different from them. He just gives you good reasons for doing things for your own benefit; it makes it hard to argue with someone when they are giving you reasons for doing something for your own benefit. *(Throughout the speech, the TEMPTER is nodding his agreement with the key points being made by the NARRATOR.)* Maybe I should get him out of here before Adam and Eve return; he's likely to cause a problem. I'm having a hard enough time keeping those two away from that tree *(as NARRATOR says this, the TEMPTER touches one piece of fruit with his finger, then another, and another until he has lightly touched each piece.)* Hey, get away from that fruit. HEY, GET OUT OF THERE! I knew he'd cause trouble! HEY, GET AWAY FROM THAT TREE! That is the tree of the fruit of the knowledge of good and evil.

TEMPTER *(loud whisper)*: I know!

NARRATOR: And no one is supposed to touch it!

TEMPTER *(with a fiendish laugh)*: HAHAHAHAHA, I KNOW! *(TEMPTER exits from one opening; ADAM enters from another.)*

ADAM: Boy, I'll never go shopping with her again!

NARRATOR *(recovering her composure after her encounter with the Tempter)*: What do you mean?

ADAM: It's Eve, she'll wear you out. God gave us hundreds of fruit trees from which to eat. Most of the fruit is just hanging there waiting to be eaten. Do you think she can make up her mind? I finally just gave up and came back here to wait *(sits down by tree)*.

TEMPTER *(from offstage, in a very loud whisper)*: Why wait?

ADAM *(to Narrator)*: What?

NARRATOR *(to Tempter offstage)*: Stop that! *(to Adam)* That wasn't me, that was . . . um. . . .

TEMPTER *(from offstage)*: Why wait? She'll take all day. And the very best fruit in the garden is right there next to you.

ADAM: Who *is* that?

NARRATOR: Ignore it, ignore it.

TEMPTER: Why wait? If you're really hungry . . .

ADAM *(to Narrator)*: Who is that? Where is that voice coming from? Am I hearing things?

NARRATOR: Yes, you are!

TEMPTER: Why wait? Why wait? Why wait?

ADAM: Why should I wait? *(walks over to the tree and picks a piece of the fruit, discovers it to be sticky, smells it, takes a little taste)*. This is a bad one. *(ADAM picks another piece as EVE enters.)*

NARRATOR: Oh, no!

EVE: Adam, what are you doing?

ADAM: I was going to eat a piece of this fruit while I was waiting for you, here *(he offers EVE first piece of fruit; she backs off)*. HERE, try it *(she takes it)*.

EVE *(sampling the fruit)*: This doesn't taste good.

ADAM: Let's try another piece *(both ADAM and EVE walk over to different members of the audience and with some difficulty manage to give their sticky fruit to the audience; both go back to the tree and pick the rest of the fruit)*.

NARRATOR *(with despair)*: Oh, no . . .

ADAM *(quickly sampling one piece of fruit after another)*: None of this is any good.

EVE *(giving a piece to NARRATOR)*: I don't like it.

ADAM: Rotten fruit! *(with difficulty he manages to get each piece unstuck; then he tosses each piece to a different member of the audience; then ADAM walks over to the tree and knocks it down.)*

TEMPTER *(in a loud voice that could be the voice of God, speaks from offstage)*: WHO IS RESPONSIBLE FOR THIS?

NARRATOR *(leaning despairingly with one arm on her lectern while holding up the piece of fruit and looking at it, she says with irony in her voice)*: That's a sticky question!

LIGHTS OUT, ALL EXIT.

(Permission is granted to make additional copies of this play for use in the local church.)

Ed Heuer is Minister of Education in the First Baptist Church of Hyattsville, Maryland.

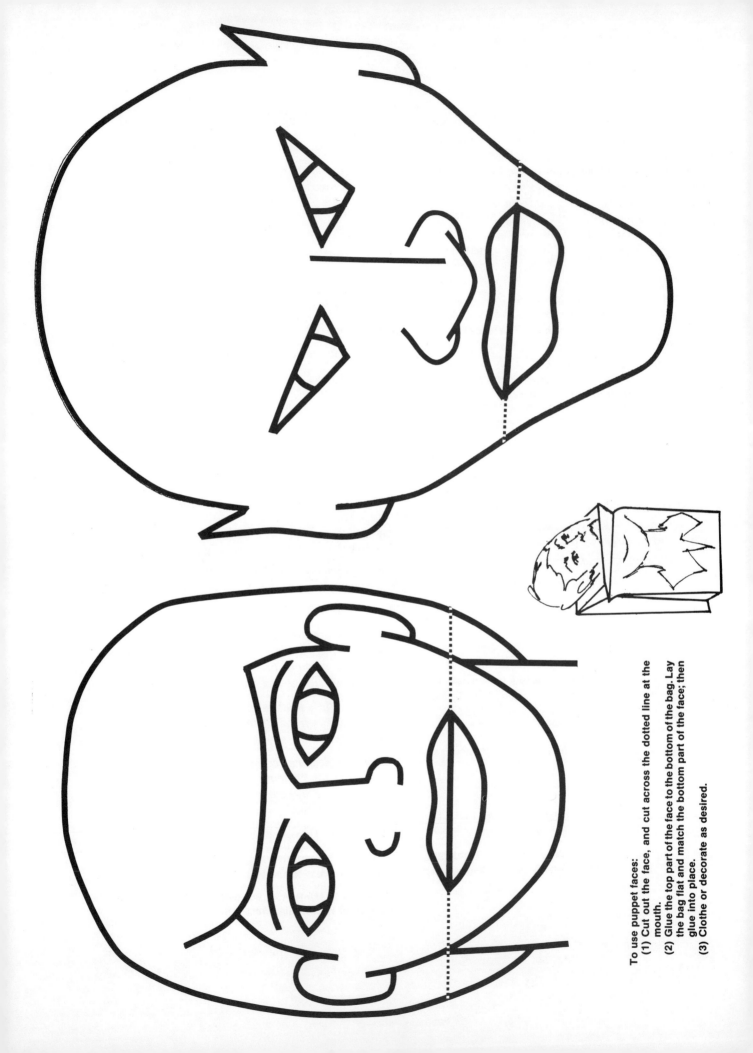

To use puppet faces:
(1) Cut out the face, and cut across the dotted line at the mouth.

(2) Glue the top part of the face to the bottom of the bag. Lay the bag flat and match the bottom part of the face; then glue into place.

(3) Clothe or decorate as desired.

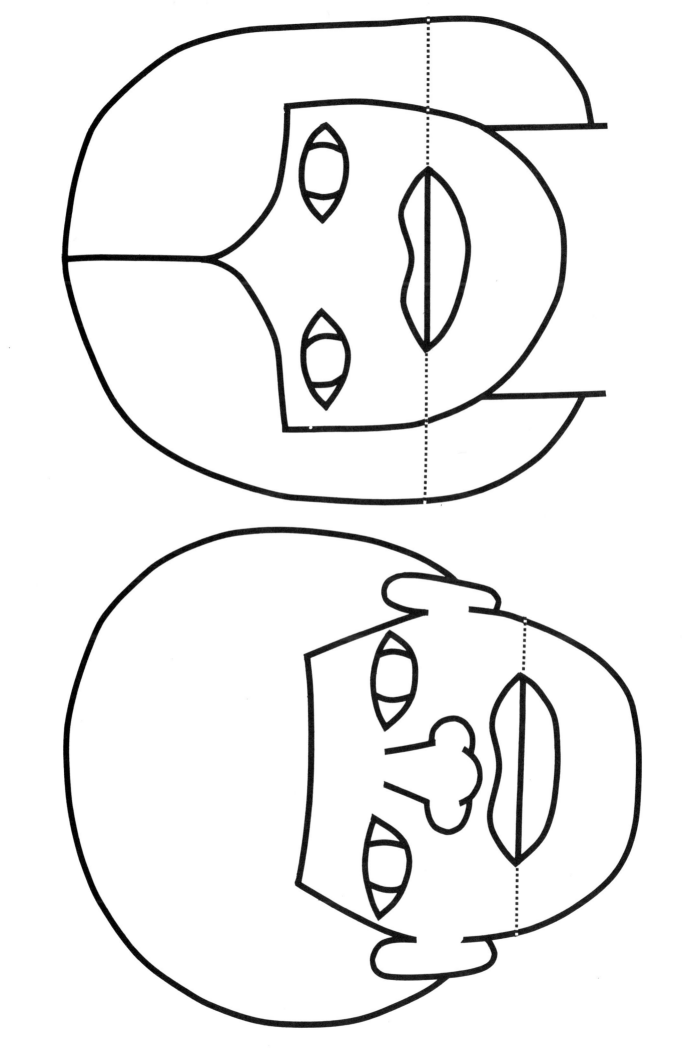

WHAT IS MISSION?

by Ronald E. Cary

GOAL: To gain an understanding of the different aspects of international mission work.

INTRODUCTION

This session is based on a filmstrip entitled *Mission is. . . .* Participants should be challenged to see the many dimensions of mission work. This and the next session are designed for small intergenerational groups (12 to 18 people), something like classes in a school of missions. The smaller groups will come together occasionally, as in this session, to view a filmstrip.

PREPARATION
You will need:

1. An hour
2. A room large enough for the total group to view the filmstrip, and either separate rooms for smaller intergenerational groups or spaces around the large room
3. Two or three worktables for each of the intergenerational groups
4. Name tags and pins, newsprint, felt-tip pens, and pencils, posterboard, crayons, magazines, scissors, and glue
5. "Sentence Completion" sheets—make one copy for each person. See Procedure Section I for sample.
6. Bibles for each small group
7. Filmstrip entitled *Mission is . . .* (available from Friendship Press or your denominational film library)
   filmstrip projector and screen
8. A general coordinator to—
   • see that work materials are available to the group leaders.
   • arrange for showing filmstrip and any other total functions that occur during the four sessions
   • train leaders
9. One or two leaders/facilitators for each intergenerational small group.

Things to do ahead of time

1. Each small-group leader will need to care for arranging the work area for his or her group.
   • Write out the purpose for the session on newsprint so that everyone can read it. Leave this taped to the wall throughout the sessions as a reminder of what the group has learned.
   • Gather the materials necessary for your group ahead of time *or* know where to direct your group members to get the necessary materials (for example, a central resource center available to all groups).
2. The general coordinator should set up chairs in a large room and have the filmstrip ready for showing when the small-group members arrive.

Publicity

1. Through the church newsletter, Sunday bulletin, or posters, inform the congregation about this experience ahead of time. Describe the experience as fully as you can.
2. Try to have advance registration of participants so that you can make each small group as fully intergenerational as possible.

PROCEDURE AND TIMING
Opening the gathering (15 minutes)

Getting to know each other in small groups:
1. As persons come into the room, ask them to—
   a. put their names on tags
   b. choose a color that best represents how they feel right now, and write the color below their name. (adults can help non-writers)
2. After a few minutes, gather everyone present into a circle and ask them to share the color they chose and the reason for choosing it.
3. Hand out the sentence completion sheets and ask everyone to respond in writing to the question listed. (again writers can help nonwriters)
   Collect these sheets when completed and give to the general coordinator.

SENTENCE COMPLETION

"From this intergenerational course on missions, I hope to learn . . ."

(Check one or more.)

[ ] about missionaries and their work.

[ ] about the places where we do mission work.

[ ] what the Bible has to say about our mission in the world.

[ ] about our reasons for mission work.

[ ] about other people in my group.

[ ] (write whatever you want here) _____
_____
_____
_____
_____

---

4. Outlining the session
- Invite someone to read the Bible verses for the session, Matthew 25:31-40.
- Share the theme and the purpose for this experience.

Developing the experience (25 minutes)

1. Send the group to see the filmstrip entitled *Mission is. . . .* Pair them in teams, an adult with a youth or a child, and ask them to notice the different kinds of mission work they see portrayed in the filmstrip. One suggestion to offer is to write down the kinds of mission work they think most important or the kind of work they would most like to do if they were missionaries.

2. At the conclusion of the filmstrip (8 minutes), the groups are to return quickly to their rooms.

3. When group members return to the room, the leaders will solicit their response to the filmstrip. It is a good idea to write these responses out on newsprint or a chalkboard. Group leaders should be especially sensitive to younger children. Tape responses listed on newsprint to the wall so that members can refer to them. Anything placed on the walls will help give the group a sense of "ownership."

Closing the gathering (20 minutes)

1. Today's session will close with an art activity. Today and next session the group members will make posters that depict one aspect of the themes for either this session *or* the next session, "What Is Mission?" *or* "Why Are We Involved in Mission?"

2. Bring together two or three of the teams created earlier to become work groups of four to six people. Then, each small group is to decide on and do the following:

   a. Choose a message or symbol that depicts the "what" or "why" of mission work. For example, a short verse of Scripture, the words "Go ye . . .," a picture of a tractor, a medical symbol, a stalk of wheat, or a picture of a globe surrounded by pictures of mission.

   b. Draw a design for the poster so the group can see how it will look. Then, decide as a group who will do which parts and start in!

REMIND EVERYONE TO BRING A BIBLE FOR THE NEXT SESSION.

Ronald E. Cary is Minister of Education in the First Baptist Church of Ann Arbor, Michigan, and Campus Minister at the University of Michigan.

WHY ARE WE INVOLVED IN MISSION?

by Ronald E. Cary

GOAL: To consider some biblical and humanitarian reasons for our involvement in mission.

INTRODUCTION

Participants should be challenged to expand their thoughts on the need for mission involvement. They will build on the experience from the previous session by continuing their art activity. The intergenerational groups or classes will be composed of the same persons as the last session.

PREPARATION
You will need:

1. The same time and space as the previous session
2. Newsprint and felt-tip pens; paper and pencils
3. A newsprint sheet with these Scripture references listed:
   Matthew 25:31-40
   John 4:7-14
   Acts 17:26-28
   Romans 1:14-16
   Romans 10:14-15
   Galatians 3:26-28
   Ephesians 2:13-22
   2 Timothy 1:6-8
   Hebrews 12:1
   Sayings of Jesus that might apply:
   The Golden Rule, Luke 6:31-35
   The house on solid ground, Luke 6:47-49
   Jesus sending out the seventy, Luke 10:1-2
   The Great Commandment, Luke 10:25-27
4. Work sheets—make two copies for each group from the sample given.
5. The same art materials as in the previous session.
6. Leadership remains the same as in the last session.

Things to do ahead of time

Write out the purpose for the session on newsprint and tape it to the wall.

PROCEDURE AND TIMING
Opening the gathering (5 minutes)

1. Begin the session with a prayer for those who are involved in mission work at home and abroad. Pray that we might discover our own roles both as "missionaries" and in support of others who go out from us to serve.
2. Briefly indicate the theme and purpose for today's session.

Developing the experience (35 minutes)

1. Brainstorming: Explain to the group that brainstorming is a process of listing responses to a question or problem without considering whether the responses are good or bad. Whatever comes to mind is acceptable. No discussion is allowed. The goal is to get as many responses to the question as possible.
2. Divide into two smaller groups, and for three minutes brainstorm answers to the question "Why are we involved in mission?"
3. Ask for a recorder in each group to take a sheet of newsprint and list all the responses of group members. Try to encourage everyone to respond, especially the children. You might have some ideas of your own written down in advance in case the process bogs down. Remember, *no discussion.* Just list the ideas!
4. After three minutes, the two groups should stop and each choose two responses they think are most interesting or most valid as reasons for our involvement in mission work.
5. Pass out two Work Sheets to each group and ask them to complete one for each response.

6. Ask the recorders to be ready to share their groups' findings on one of the two responses with the total group.
7. Call the whole group back together. Have the recorders share their findings on *one* of the two responses. Tape the report sheets to the wall so that everyone can read them.
8. Conclude the discussion by suggesting that individuals or families might take some of the other ideas about mission home with them and follow the same process there as a family activity.
9. Remind members of the group of the many different kinds of mission work carried on today, and for many different reasons. Ask them to set aside a time to remember missionaries in their prayers and to pray for a personal sense of mission in their own lives.

Closing the gathering (20 minutes)

1. In the time remaining, continue working on the poster begun last session. There will be some time in the next two sessions to put the finishing touches on the posters.

Ronald E. Cary is Minister of Education in the First Baptist Church of Ann Arbor, Michigan, and Campus Pastor at the University of Michigan.

WORK SHEET

1. Reason for mission involvement: _____

_____

2. Why is this a good reason? Are there any negative aspects to consider? _____

_____

_____

3. Is there a biblical basis for this reason? Can you think of a particular passage that would apply?

_____

_____

(See the list of Scripture references that has been posted if you need ideas.)

4. In what ways could we personally fulfill this reason? Is there something we could do here at home?

_____

_____

_____

(Use this space for additional responses.)

WHERE DOES MISSION TAKE PLACE?— PART ONE

by Ronald E. Cary

GOAL: To gain a broad perspective on the global mission of the church and to learn something about the specific places where mission work is carried out.

INTRODUCTION

Through the use of information and study material from the overseas mission arm of your denomination, participants will gain some insight into the global dimensions of mission work, while specifically studying one location of your denomination's international ministry.

PREPARATION
You will need:

1. An overall coordinator and a number of small-group helpers to assist in the study of the mission areas
2. An hour and a room large enough for a number of small groups to work together on a mission map (for example, a large multipurpose room or fellowship hall area)
3. Name tags, pencils, and paper
4. "Sentence Completion" response sheets—make a copy for each person from the sample provided.
5. Mission location work sheets—make copies for each group from the sample provided.
6. Denominational mission study materials (order from your own denomination's overseas mission agency)
7. Mission map instruction sheet—make copies for each group from the sample provided.
8. Plywood or posterboard mission map (8′ x 4′ suggested size)
9. Plywood or posterboard squares (8″ or 9″ suggested size)
10. Paintbrushes (for both painting and lettering)
11. As many different colors of poster paint as there are countries where your denomination is at work
12. Black and white paint or markers (for lettering)
13. Old newspapers

Things to do ahead of time

1. Sometime during the week preceding this session, divide participants into groups of three. Give each group of three a number. Make name tags for each one with his or her group number written on it. Make sure that each group of three has at least one adult in it.
2. Write out the purpose of this session on newsprint.
3. Construct a large wall map of the world (8′ x 4′). With the help of a pantograph and someone skilled in woodcutting, the shapes of the continents or major countries could be cut out of cheap plywood. An alternative would be to cut the continents and countries out of heavy posterboard. Keeping the map to scale will give it a more "professional" appearance. The continents and countries should be mounted on a heavy piece of wood with a blue background. If continents and/or countries are fastened to the mounting board with wood screws, they can be removed individually. The whole board should be permanently affixed to a large wall, perhaps in a mission room or fellowship hall.
4. Cut out enough plywood squares or posterboard squares to serve as a "key" to the particular mission locations you'll be studying.
5. Choose a different color of paint for each particular mission location.
6. Use black and white paint or markers for lettering on the plywood "keys."
7. All of the items connected with the construction of the mission map should be set up ahead of time in a large work area. Old newspapers should be used to cover table tops. Everything should be well-organized so that group members can go right to their mission location and find:
   a. the continent or country
   b. paint and paintbrushes
   c. plywood or posterboard squares

Publicity

If group members have finished their posters, you

might hang them in a place where all the church members can see them. Indicate that these have been made by members of the intergenerational mission study group.

PROCEDURE AND TIMING
Opening the gathering (20 minutes)

1. It is good to allow members of the group to express feelings about what is going on, especially the children in the group. This exercise will help to do it.
2. As people arrive, ask them to pick up their name tags, a "Sentence Completion" response sheet, and a pencil. Ask them to complete the sentence "Right now I feel this intergenerational group on missions has been. . . ." (examples: ". . . fun," ". . . all right", ". . . a waste of time," etc.)

SENTENCE COMPLETION

"Right now I feel this intergenerational group on missions has been . . ."

Check one and/or add your own.

[ ] fantastic.
[ ] very interesting.
[ ] good.
[ ] not so good.
[ ] boring.
[ ] a waste of time.
[ ] other _____

Note: This is voluntary. You don't have to answer if you don't want to.

---

3. You might have to explain that the purpose of the response sheet is to help people think how they feel about the group so far. Let everyone know that this is voluntary. They don't have to write anything down if they don't want to.
4. When all members have arrived and finished with the response sheet, ask them to join the other two people who have the same number they do. They are to take a few minutes to share their response with the others. (Make sure there is an adult in each triad that contains young children.)
5. After a few minutes, gain the attention of the total group and explain the theme and purpose of the session. (This will also be the theme for the final session): "Our goal is to study different areas of mission work and to complete a large 'mission map' that will be permanently fixed on the wall in (fellowship hall). This map will be surrounded by the posters that we've been working on. Our international mission work occurs in many places. We will study those places that you choose. We will not consider mission work in our own country at this time."

Developing the experience (40 minutes)

1. Put each mission location on a sheet of newsprint. Put these in different areas of the room and invite each group of three to choose and then go to the mission area they want to study.
   • If two groups choose the same mission location to study, let them work together as a group of six.
   • If a third group chooses that same area to study, ask that group to make a second choice. It's best if no more than six persons study a particular mission field.
2. When groups are settled, the small group leaders assigned to each mission area can pass out the study material you have gathered and the mission work sheets. Small-group leaders will then encourage looking for both words and pictures that tell about the mission field, and they will help group members to share their findings with one another. The group may want to look over the map and identify the location of the country assigned to them. One of the younger members might be assigned immediately to paint both the country and the square.

**MISSION LOCATION
WORK SHEET**

(For use with Session Number Three and with Mission Packets)

Mission location:

List the kinds of work done in this location.

List the names and skills of missionaries in this location (if information is available).

List some of the needs particular to this location (i.e., water for irrigation, medical supplies, books, etc.)

---

3. Pass out Mission Map Instruction Sheets to each group.

MISSION MAP INSTRUCTION SHEET

Our wall map is located in (Fellowship Hall). It comes in two parts: the continent or section of the world in which your mission location exists and a small plywood square that will serve as a "key" to briefly describe something about that location.

You are to do the following:
1. Get a container of poster paint that has been assigned to your mission location.
2. Paint your location on the wall map.
3. Paint a plywood square the same color.
4. The plywood square will serve as a "key" to your location. It should contain as much of the following information as your group deems necessary:
   a. name of country or location;
   b. symbols of our work in that location (i.e., tractor for agriculture, red cross for medical, etc.), *or* a word for our work (medical, etc.);
   c. names of some of the missionaries;
   d. special needs of that location.

---

4. Remind them that painting the plywood square must be done during this session if it is to be dry by the next (and last) session.

Closing the gathering

The gathering will close with members in study or at work on the mission map.

Ronald E. Cary is Minister of Education in the First Baptist Church of Ann Arbor, Michigan, and University Pastor at the University of Michigan.

NASA

MISSION

WHERE DOES MISSION TAKE PLACE?— PART TWO

by Ronald E. Cary

INTRODUCTION

This session continues and concludes the activity begun in the previous session.

PREPARATION

You will need (in addition to the materials used last session):

1. Evaluation forms (See sample at end of the session outline.)
2. Copies of "A Play: Missions?" by Elizabeth Strauss.

Things to do ahead of time

1. During the week, group leaders might "touch up" any painting done last session on the map or plywood squares.
2. If you expect to use the play, prepare enough copies for the groups who will need them.

Procedure and Timing
Opening the gathering (15 minutes)

1. Begin the session with prayer for the mission of the church to spread the gospel throughout the world.
2. Briefly remind participants of the things you have studied during these sessions. Look around and recall some of the important things you have done.
3. Ask for volunteers to respond to these questions: "If I were a missionary, I would like to do (what kind of work?) in (what place in the world?)."
4. Next, pass out evaluation forms. Ask everyone to take a few minutes to fill in an evaluation form (readers help nonreaders). Collect the completed forms.

Developing the experience (40 minutes)

1. Explain that the next forty minutes are for finishing the mission map. If any of the groups finish work on the map, the group leaders can offer them the short playlet entitled, "A Play: Missions?" The play can be prepared for sharing and discussion at the close of the session.
2. If groups have not finished the posters, they can work on these as well.

Closing the gathering (15 minutes)

1. Gather the group around the mission map and mount the posters on the wall.
2. Sing a mission hymn together, such as "We've a Story to Tell to the Nations" or "In Christ There Is No East or West."
3. Join hands and offer a prayer of dedication: offer God the work you have done, and your hopes for healing, peace, and justice in the world.
4. Dismiss with this benediction: "Now *you* go into the world—every part of it—to be and do the love of God. Amen."

Ronald E. Cary is Minister of Education in the First Baptist Church of Ann Arbor, Michigan, and Campus Pastor at the University of Michigan.

EVALUATION FORM

1. How did you approach these intergenerational sessions? Circle the number that best shows your response.

   6   5   4   3   2   1   0

   with
   expectation

   with
   indifference

2. Were you interested in the topic? Circle the appropriate number.

   6   5   4   3   2   1   0

   very
   much   quite
   a bit   not
   much   not
   at all

3. Rate the way you felt about the event overall. Circle appropriate number.

   6   5   4   3   2   1   0

   excellent good fair poor very
   poor waste
   of time

4. What did you like (check one or more)—

	best?	least?
What Is Mission? (first session)	_____	
Why Mission? (second session)	_____	
Where Does Mission Take Place? (third and fourth sessions)	_____	
Working on posters	_____	
Working on mission map	_____	
Discussion times	_____	
Filmstrip *Mission Is . . .*	_____	
Getting to know others	_____	
Other _____	_____	_____

5. Would you like more intergenerational experiences? Circle one.

   yes   no

6. If your answer to the above questions was "yes," do you have any suggestions to make (i.e., themes, times, etc.)? Answer below:

   _____

   _____

   _____

   _____

A PLAY: MISSIONS?

by Elizabeth C. Strauss

(3 boys, 2 girls)

MIKE: What do you want to be when you grow up?

DOUG: A missionary.

MIKE: A missionary? What's a missionary?

DOUG: Oh, someone who goes to a foreign country.

JOHN: My father went to Holland on a business trip. Is he a missionary?

DOUG: No, I mean countries that are poor and need help.

JOHN: Like where?

DOUG: Oh, Africa or India or Alaska.

JOHN: Alaska! That's a state in the United States. It's not a poor country.

DOUG: No, but they have Eskimos.

JOHN: Are Eskimos poor?

DOUG: I don't know, but they're sort of foreign and different.

JEAN: What are you going to do when you're a missionary?

DOUG: Oh, I'll build a church and tell the people that God loves them.

JEAN: What if they're sick?

DOUG: I'll build a hospital for them, I guess.

JEAN: What if they need a job?

DOUG: Oh, well, I'll teach them how to read; then they can get a job. I'll build them a school.

LYNN: What if they're hungry?

DOUG: I'll give them food.

LYNN: Where will you get the food?

DOUG: Oh, God will provide.

LYNN: Where will you get the money to build the church and the hospital and the school?

DOUG: Hmmm—from our church, I guess.

MIKE: So, you'll tell the poor people about God and give them everything that they need. What if they don't like you?

DOUG: What! Of course they'll like me. I'm doing everything for them.

LYNN: That's just it. You're doing everything for them and they do nothing for themselves. I'd rather do it myself.

DOUG: Well, we Americans have the money and the education. And I'm willing to give up my easy life in America in order to help these poor foreign people.

JEAN: Aren't there poor people in America, too?

JOHN: Sure.

MIKE: So, you could even be a missionary in the United States of America.

DOUG: Oh, no, that's not the same as a missionary to another country.

MIKE: But if people need you here, why should you go to people far away? Besides, it doesn't look good to send missionaries from the U.S. to other countries when there are such horrible things happening here—like murder, racial prejudices, and dishonesty in the government.

DOUG: Well, really, how could I be a missionary in our state? We don't need churches or hospitals or schools here.

MIKE: No, but all people need to know that God loves them and that Christ died for them.

DOUG: Oh, but Americans know about God already. They go to church. They even give money to support missionaries.

JOHN: Americans don't act as if they know God. They cheat, steal, lie, kill, gossip, and hurt one another. I don't think that very many Americans really know God—really know and believe the teachings of Christ.

DOUG: OK. I guess you're right. Americans need missionaries as much as, if not more than, other people. But are you saying that we shouldn't try to help people in other countries?

MIKE: I don't know. What do the rest of you think?

From *Baptist Leader*, December, 1976. Used by permission of the American Baptist Board of Education and Publication.

ECOLOGY AND THE OUTDOORS

by Virgil K. and Lynn T. Nelson

GOAL: To provide opportunity for building ties between generations in mutual reflection on the ugliness, the beauty, and the interrelatedness of all life in our world.

INTRODUCTION

This session is based upon the structure of a church picnic in an out-of-doors setting. Pick a favorite place or try a new one as you plan for this event.

PREPARATION
You will need:

1. An hour in addition to eating and games time
2. An outdoors location (public, private, primitive, or plush depending on your preferences)
3. Materials: large paper sacks (one for each group of 8); a whistle; a way to make a leader's voice heard (depending on the size of your group, you may need a megaphone or perhaps a P.A. system); songsheets or chorus books; sheets with facts and litany (make copies from the sample provided); pencils (one for each group of 8); a musical instrument; Bibles marked at passages
4. Photographers and people to do a cassette tape interview for later slide-show sharing
5. One leader minimum (ideally three leaders—one to give the verbal instructions and coordinate the time flow; one to float and answer questions and encourage; another to give special talent to the music in the opening and closing times)
6. Copies of the Fact Sheet and Litany of Thanksgiving printed with this program.

Things to do ahead of time

Choose the place for the picnic; round up materials; secure leaders; publicize.

Publicity

Use phrases in bulletins and on posters, such as: "It's a Small World," "Subdue the Earth," "Spaceship Earth," "Co-Residents Together," "He's Got the Whole World in His Hands."

Additional Resources

1. *99 Ways to a Simple Life-Style,* Albert Fritsch, ed. Center for Science in the Public Interest, Anchor Books, 1977
2. *Taking Charge: A Process Packet for Simple Living: Personal and Social Change.* Palo Alto Packet Committee. The American Friends Service Committee of S.F. $1.25. AFSC Bookstore, 2160 Lake St., San Francisco, CA 94121
3. *Alternative Celebrations* catalog. 3rd edition. Alternatives, 701 N. Eugene St., Greensboro, NC 27401

PROCEDURE AND TIMING

- Allow ample time for people to eat.
- Announce a starting time for games and encourage participation. An excellent new resource for group games is *The New Games Book: Play Hard, Play Fair, Nobody Hurt,* edited by Andrew Fluegelman (New York: Doubleday & Co., Inc., 1976), $4.95. It has many intergenerational suggestions for good fun. Adjust the amount of time for games in light of the day's schedule, allowing one hour for the program while there is still daylight.

Opening the gathering (10 minutes)

1. Call people to assemble in a circle or semicircle on the grass. To hasten a common focus, start a familiar song.
2. Spend about five minutes in fun group singing.
3. Introduce the theme of the day: This setting provides an excellent opportunity for us to get better acquainted as individuals and as a church family; plus, the setting itself is ideal for looking at our relationship to the planet Earth which supports our lives. We want to spend some time getting better acquainted, working in groups rediscovering the

beauty of God's earth, and, at the end recommitting ourselves as caretakers of the earth.

Grouping (10 minutes)

1. We're going to divide the group in half. All persons whose birthdays are January through June will be on one side; all July through December on the other. Now find the person whose birthday is closest to yours (allow 3–4 minutes).
2. With your birthday-close mate (in twos) share one memory you have of a picnic (2 minutes). Then, let the leader choose one of the following for each pair to share further (2 minutes):

   "I am more like—a river or a stream?

               —a tree or a cactus?

               —sandstone or granite?"
3. Now find a couple having quite differing ages from yours and make a foursome. Be sure you know first names. Each person shares one thing he or she learned about his or her partner (3 minutes).

Developing the experience (30 minutes)

1. "Sack stash": We are going to play a game vital to the survival of our planet: "Sack Stash." Each group of four finds another group of four. Get a length of rope and a paper sack (2 minutes).

   • Each team of eight has to hold onto the rope at all times while moving around to see which team can pick up the most evidence of human activity in this area. If anyone lets go of the rope, then the team must start over again. You have five minutes.

   • Keep track of your own points on this basis: two points for each item which is evidence of our group here today; one point for each item from other people who have been here.

   • The leader will blow a whistle when it's time to reassemble. Move as far as you can. Go!

   • After five minutes, blow the whistle. Take three minutes to ascertain point totals. Cheer the "sack stash local champions."

   • As each team reports its score, hand out the fact sheet, several copies to each group.
2. Reflection (10 minutes). Sit together in the same group of eight and talk about:

   • Why were you able to find what you put in your sack? Why didn't you find certain items? (Possible reasons: availability of trash cans, people who don't care, habit, consumerism—use of disposable items.)

   • Have someone in the group read aloud each fact statement; pause for comments.

3. Senses walk (10 minutes): Divide into twosomes to lead one another in a blindfolded sense walk.

   • Explain that when our dominant sense of sight is taken away, we experience the other senses more strongly.

   • One leads the blindfolded person to different places to smell, feel, hear, and even taste the things around. Whistle for a switch in leadership after five minutes; the leader then gets led blindfolded. Yes, a child can lead an adult!
4. Reflection. Bring pairs together to form a foursome and share in response to these questions: What did I learn or relearn about myself? About the earth?
5. Optionals (To create an extra half hour of program or to substitute for activities above).

   • In a foursome, share one place on the earth which you would like to see remain unchanged for all time (5 minutes).

   • In eights, invite each person to select something within sight, think about how it relates to his or her faith, then share (10 to 15 minutes).

   • Give a Scripture passage (see those listed with the closing worship) to each group of eight for them to meditate upon, discuss, and decide how to present to the rest of the group (chant, cheer, pantomime, song, skit, or choral reading) (20 to 30 minutes).

Closing the gathering (10 minutes)

1. Gather the total group with a familiar song, such as "For the Beauty of the Earth."
2. Invite all to silent prayer and then share aloud evidences of God's beauty on earth (phrases or sentences from those who wish).
3. Ask several people to read aloud the following Scriptures: Genesis 1:28-31; Genesis 2:4-5; Psalm 8; Jeremiah 12:4. Encourage quiet during and between each message from God.
4. In twosomes share one thing you could do to improve as caretaker of the earth. What could the church do?
5. Invite any who wish to share their commitments to be better caretakers of the earth. Invite all to search their hearts and life-styles and to make a commitment to grow as God's caretakers of the earth.
6. Lead the Litany of Thanksgiving (printed on the fact sheet) or ask for spontaneous phrases.
7. Close with a song: "Father, We Thank Thee"; "He's Got the Whole World in His Hands."

Virgil K. Nelson and Lynn T. Nelson of Ventura, California, are Consultants in Christian Education.

SOME FACTS[1]

1. Did you know that if you drink two cans of soda in aluminum cans and fail to recycle the cans, you have wasted more energy than one billion people in the world use in a total day?
2. The U.S. and Canada are 6 percent of the world's population; yet we use over half the world's raw materials and 33 percent of the world's energy. The World Wildlife Fund estimates that we overeat by 30 percent and produce in the process over 100 pounds of garbage per person per year.
3. It takes 460 pounds of coal to burn a 60-watt light bulb continuously for one year.
4. The relative consumption of the earth's energy resources per year:

USA	9728	Energy Units*
Canada	8314	E. U.
Sweden	4915	E. U.
China	550	E. U.
India	170	E. U.
Haiti/Ethiopia	26	E. U.

*To drive a Buick (15 mpg) 10 miles takes 3 E.U.'s.

[1]Items 1, 3, and 4 are taken from Anne Pierotti and Albert J. Fritsch, *Lifestyle Index—76* (Washington, D.C.: Center for Science in the Public Interest, 1976), pp. 14, 20, 46, and 37 respectively.

LITANY OF THANKSGIVING

Following each petition all will say: "Let us give thanks to God, for his steadfast love endures forever." (Shorten this to "Let us give thanks to God" if your group has quite a few youngsters.)

Start with:

—For the gift of life: *Let us give thanks to God* . . .
—For the earth and water and sun which support and sustain us: *Let us* . . .
—For the Son, who demonstrated a new way to live and who calls us into the struggle against evil to establish his kingdom of love and justice on earth; *Let us* . . .
—For the varied experiences of youth and maturity: *Let us* . . .
—For faith which makes the impossible seem possible: *Let us* . . .
—For courage which seems to come exactly when we need it: *Let us give* . . .
—For laughter, which is our best defense against despair: *Let us give* . . .
—For each other, who believe and hope and love and work and laugh and sing and serve together: *Let us* . . .

Encourage people to make up additional phrases.

Camerique

79

MISSION

DINOSAURS

by Donald T-M Ng

GOAL: To understand better the Christian's approach to today's energy problems.

INTRODUCTION

Being rich in natural resources and technological skills, America has had the privilege of achieving almost any material goal it set. Like a shopper with an unlimited credit card, Americans sometimes take their high standards of living for granted without the full awareness of how it is for human communities in other parts of the world. Americans use more energy than any other country in the world. At the same time, Americans represent only a fraction of the world's total population. This gross imbalance between American consumption and world energy supplies is due to real ignorance of the worldwide need for conservation of energy, for cooperation, and for interdependence among all the world's peoples. There is no way America can continue to consume energy at its present lavish levels, even with high-priced foreign oil, stepped-up domestic oil production, and new energy technologies. Energy shortages will be a part of life unless we learn about conservation.

During the past several winters, many have experienced firsthand the importance of conservation. In 1977, meteorologists in Ohio reported twenty record-breaking lows, making it the coldest winter since 1876. With temperatures averaging ten degrees below normal in December, 1976, Michigan suffered through its worst winter of the century.

Energy is necessary for living. This session will enable the participants to explore the Christian's approach to energy through Bible study, by looking at current events, and by using creative arts.

PREPARATION
You will need:

1. One hour
2. A large room where tables and chairs can be spaced about for each group of six or so
3. Bibles, Bible commentaries and dictionaries, paper, pencils, magazines, newspapers, glue, scissors, felt-tip markers, large newsprint or butcher paper, masking tape, construction paper for name tags, small toy dinosaurs
4. Hymnbooks and a musical instrument
5. One leader to introduce the session and to guide the development of the exercises. (The leader needs to be someone who is sensitive to global concerns.)

Things to do ahead of time

1. Make name tags by cutting 8½" x 11" construction paper in fourths.
2. Prepare a large piece of paper by taping together two pieces of butcher paper or taping together a number of sheets of poster-size newsprint. Draw the outline of a dinosaur on it.

3. Write all instructions for name tags on newsprint for people to see when they arrive. List the Bible references on newsprint.
4. Set up the room.

Publicity

On posters, in a mailing, or on a bulletin insert, describe the program as an intergenerational event. For eye-catchers, use: "Come decorate a dinosaur!" or "Where Have All the Dinosaurs Gone, Long Time Passing?"

PROCEDURE AND TIMING
Opening the gathering (10 minutes)

1. As people arrive, they can make name tags according to the instructions posted:
   (a) Write your name in BIG letters at the top of the tag.
   (b) Under your name, list the many things you use in the course of the day that consume energy.
2. Readers and writers help nonreaders and nonwriters. Children may wish to draw pictures of energy-

using things: lamp, car, TV, toaster, record player.

3. Invite the participants to mill around to get to know one another. Share where you use the most energy in an average day.

Developing the experience (40 minutes)

1. Divide into groups of six with two adults, two youth, and two children in each group if possible. You may need to make the groups larger or smaller by one person. Avoid having only one child or youth in a group of adults. Parents can accompany a child less than eight years old. Ask groups to choose a table where they can work.

2. Allow some time for each member of the small groups to share for a minute about himself or herself.

3. Introduce the session as an opportunity to learn what God says about energy, to become informed on the current energy situation, and to work creatively together on what we can do about it. As the leader, share an experience of how the energy crisis has affected your life.

4. Refer to the list of biblical references posted on the wall. Ask each group to look up the references. Provide Bibles, commentaries, dictionaries, paper, and pencils.

   References:
   Genesis 1:26-31—interdependence of plants, animals, and humankind
   Genesis 8:20-22—dependability of God's world
   Psalm 8—our place in God's world
   Psalm 24:1-2—the earth is the Lord's
   Psalm 65:9-13—the blessing of rain
   Psalm 104—the plan of the world
   Isaiah 55—God offers good things to all

5. Questions for discussion in the small groups:
   - What is our human responsibility for God's creation?
   - What is God's plan for the world?
   - Does God plan for shortages?
   - What are our responsibilities for others' energy needs?

6. After the Bible study period, ask each group to come up with a *slogan* that describes the group's feeling on the energy problem.

7. Gather the entire group together around the large poster of the dinosaur, laid on the floor. Invite each group to share its slogan. "What were some of the reasons for such a slogan?" Ask the groups to write the slogans here and there on the dinosaur.

8. Pass out copies of current magazines and newspapers to each person. Ask them to cut out articles and pictures that have relevance to energy. Invite the participants to read parts of an article or share a picture that they have found with their group before gluing it on the dinosaur. This may be an informal fun time of learning and sharing with each other.

9. After the dinosaur is covered with slogans, pictures, and articles, invite the total group to suggest ways they can conserve more energy. By this time the participants should have a better understanding of the energy needs of the world and ways we can do something about it. List the conservation tips on the blank margins of the dinosaur poster.

Closing the gathering (10 minutes)

1. Have your dinosaur poster hung up in a place where others may see it.

2. Form a large circle. Invite people to share what they have learned about energy today. Sing "All Things Bright and Beautiful" or "This Is My Father's World."

3. Close either with a personal prayer which summarizes the highlights of the session or use this benediction:

   "The earth is the Lord's and the
     fulness thereof,
   the world and those who dwell therein. . . ."
   "Now may the Lord of peace himself give you peace at all times in all ways.
   The Lord be with you all"
                    (Psalm 24:1-2; 2 Thessalonians 3:16).

4. Pass out little toy dinosaurs as souvenirs of the event.

Donald T-M Ng is a member of the staff of the Department of Ministry with Youth of the American Baptist Churches.

MISSION

COME TO MY HOUSE

by Donald T-M Ng

GOAL: To experience the richness of God's multicultural world.

INTRODUCTION

In our shrinking world today, we cannot afford to isolate ourselves from others. Rather, recognizing our interdependence as a world community, we need to pool our ideas, skills, and resources to make our world a better place to live. Gone are the days when any one people can use all the fuel they want, or consume all the food they can eat, or remain ignorant of what's going on politically, economically, or socially in another part of the world. *We* need *them. They* need *us. We* need *each other.*

In the Old Testament, the different tribes of Israel were given special responsibilities to preserve the well-being of the whole. Some were priests to care for the ark of the covenant; some were farmers to raise food; others were soldiers to ward off attackers. They functioned to meet each other's needs and were joined together by their religious faith in God.

Today we can learn from the Old Testament Hebrew life-style of mutual responsibility. In almost every community in America, there is a richness of cultural and racial pluralism for us to discover and appreciate. In many local churches, the composition of the congregation contains a variety of cultural and ethnic backgrounds, reflecting the larger community around the church. This session enables participants to take a look at their cultural heritages and to share them in a heterogeneous group. As the result of this experience, they may grow to learn and appreciate God's multicultural world.

PREPARATION
You will need:
1. One and one-half hours
2. A large carpeted room where tables and chairs can be spaced about for each family unit
3. Large pieces of newsprint or butcher paper, colored construction paper, cardboard, glue, Scotch Tape, masking tape, scissors, felt-tip markers, pencils, pipe cleaners, string, name tags made from construction paper
4. Songbooks and a musical instrument
5. One leader to introduce the session, to encourage and support the discussion, and to keep time (the person would be more effective if he or she has convictions about the positive values of intercultural/racial understanding).

Things to do ahead of time
1. Make name tags by cutting 8½" x 11" construction paper into fourths.
2. Print the six questions for the family tree activity on newsprint. Print name tag instructions on newsprint and attach a sample name tag.
3. Lay out sets of materials for each family unit at the session: some construction paper, cardboard, glue, tape, scissors, felt-tip markers, pencils, pipe cleaners, and string.
4. Arrange the room with a center area for the entire group to meet and share, and surrounding areas with tables and chairs to allow families to work individually.

Publicity
1. Publicize the event in the church paper, Sunday bulletins, and posters around the church as an opportunity to get to know people of different cultural backgrounds.
2. Prepare a fact sheet on the event with a "tear off" registration form to be turned in to you. Have a place to indicate the number of persons who will attend.
3. Examine the list of registered participants to determine if there is a variety of cultural backgrounds represented prior to the scheduled event.
4. If the registered participants are not as varied as you wish that they were, you may want to extend a

personal invitation to certain persons to come.

5. If more diversity is desired, ask your pastor to contact a church of a different cultural background from yours and invite members of that congregation to participate.

PROCEDURE AND TIMING
Opening the gathering (10 minutes)

1. As people arrive, have them fill in a name tag.
2. Help the nonwriters to make name tags also.
3. Gather the entire group and tell them the theme is: "Come to My House." The time we spend together will be an opportunity to share ourselves, our families, and our homes. In the course of the session, we will get the chance to work as families and to interact with one another in order to foster better intercultural understanding.
4. Invite any questions that the participants may have regarding the content of the session.
5. Now, for the purpose of getting to know one another, find three persons to sign your name tag in this order:
    (a) one who is younger than you
    (b) one who is older than you
    (c) one whom you don't know

Developing the experience (70 minutes)

1. Ask the people to gather together as family units and to choose a table or a space on the floor to work. Ask single persons to gather together as a group. Invite the group of single persons to share briefly about themselves.
2. Explain to the groups that in families, you will create a family tree. Each single person will work alone reflecting on his or her family experiences. Encourage the family groups to be sure each person has a chance to contribute to the creation of the family tree. Children may fill in those areas which call for a picture or drawing.
3. Hand out a large sheet of newsprint to each of the family units. Give single persons each a sheet of newsprint.
    • Ask each of the groups or persons to draw on the newsprint a "family tree" with roots, a trunk, branches, buds, leaves, and fruit.
    • Invite the participants to answer the six questions (posted on the wall) on their newsprint trees.
    1) On the roots of the tree, list the geographical areas your ancestors were from: i.e., cities, regions, countries, etc.

2) On the trunk of the tree, write your last name. Define the meaning of your last name or what it means to you with words or a drawing.
3) On the branches, draw three things you have done together as a family in the past year.
4) What is something, as a family, for which you are striving? Or looking forward to? Draw or write it on the buds.
5) What are you most proud about as a family? Draw or write it on the leaves.
6) As a family, what do you regard as your family's greatest achievement? Draw or write it on the fruit.

4. After everyone is finished, gather group members in the center of the room to share their family trees. Invite each person and group to share a part of their tree.
    • As the leader, highlight both the varieties and similarities of experiences expressed. Help the group to see that people generally have similar concerns and hopes for their lives.
    • Post the family trees around the room.
5. Explain to the group that as families and persons, we live in an interdependent world. If we didn't have each other, we would not be able to ask our

neighbors for a cup of sugar, or have neighbors watch out for our homes when we are away, or have other children on the street for our children to play with.

• Love for our neighbor is one of the great commandments of Jesus. In order to dramatize this point, ask each of the families and persons to return to their work areas.

6. Pass out to each group the collection of materials you set up earlier.

• Explain to the participants that their task is to construct a replica of their homes or apartments with the given materials.

• The replicas may be as detailed or as simple as the participants choose.

• Children may work on small models of furniture, family cars, toys, while the adults may work on the structure of the building.

• The leader may spend this time to construct a replica of the local church.

7. After the constructions are completed, gather all the replicas together and arrange them on the floor as a neighborhood. Place your model of the church in the center of the other models.

• Invite each person and family group to say something briefly about their homes. Share with the group that this is a symbol of having people "come into your home."

Closing the gathering (10 minutes)

1. Standing in a circle surrounding the model neighborhood, invite the participants to share what they have learned about themselves, about others, about the multicultural world of which we are members.

2. Invite the group to join hands to sing: "We Are One in the Spirit."

3. Close either with a personal prayer which summarizes the session activities or with the benediction· "May the God of steadfastness and encouragement grant you to live in such harmony with one another, in accord with Christ Jesus, that together you may with one voice glorify the God and Father of our Lord Jesus Christ" (Romans 15:5-6).

Donald T-M Ng is a member of the staff of the Department of Ministry with Youth of the American Baptist Churches.

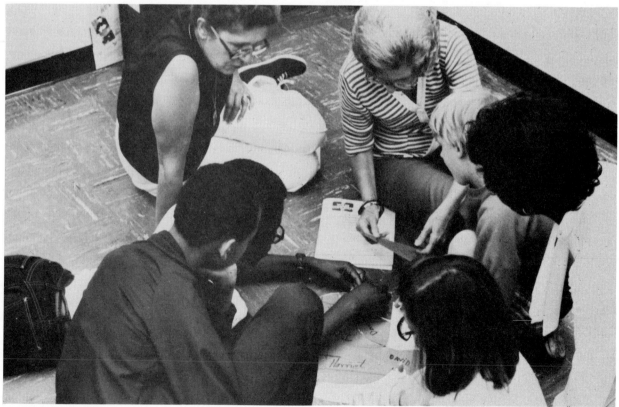

Joe Leonard

A BIBLICAL FAMILY

by Elizabeth Wright Gale

GOAL: To enter into some of the experiences of Jacob's family through the media of music and storytelling.

INTRODUCTION

The stories of Jacob and his family are among the best known and loved of all Bible stories. The purpose of this session is not to study the details of the story but to experience some parts of the story on a feeling level.

PREPARATION
You will need:

1. Construction paper and pins, markers or crayons
2. A recording of "Joseph and the Amazing Technicolor Dreamcoat," available on MCA records, #399. (Perhaps someone in the congregation owns this album. If not, try your public library or a record store, if you wish to buy it.)
3. A good record player
4. The words and music of "Joseph and the Amazing Technicolor Dreamcoat" by Andrew Lloyd Webber and Tim Rice, published by Novello Publications, Inc., 145 Palisade Street, Dobbs Ferry, NY 10522

Things to do ahead of time

1. Prepare name tags in twelve different colors and/or shapes at least 4″ x 6″. Print in small letters the name of each of the children of Jacob (the twelve tribes of Israel) on each tag of the same color or shape. Make about the same number of tags for each tribal name.
2. Prepare cards with excerpts of Jacob's predictions about each of his sons (Genesis 49, TEV), one name to a card, as follows:
   REUBEN—"you are the proudest and strongest of all my sons. You are like a raging flood" (see Genesis 49:3-4).
   SIMEON and LEVI—"they killed men in anger. I will scatter them throughout the land of Israel" (see Genesis 49:5-8).
   JUDAH—"your brothers will praise you and bow down before you. You will hold the royal scepter and nations will bring you tribute" (see Genesis 49:8-12).
   ZEBULUN—"will live beside the sea. His shore will be a haven for ships" (see Genesis 49:13).
   ISSACHAR—"is no better than a donkey that lies stretched out between its saddlebags . . . and is forced to work as a slave" (see Genesis 49:14-15).
   DAN—"a snake at the side of the road . . . that strikes at the horse's heel, so that the rider is thrown off backward" (see Genesis 49:16-18).
   GAD—"will be attacked by a band of robbers, but he will turn and pursue them" (see Genesis 49:19).
   ASHER—"his land will produce rich food . . . fit for a king" (see Genesis 49:20).
   NAPHTALI—"is a deer that runs free, who bears lovely fawns" (see Genesis 49:21).
   JOSEPH—"is like a wild donkey by a spring" (see Genesis 49:22-26).
   BENJAMIN—"is like a vicious wolf, morning and evening he kills and devours" (see Genesis 49:27).
3. Choose an expert storyteller and a song leader and go over plans for the session with them. Decide which parts of the story will be told, which will be sung, and which will be heard on the record. If you cannot secure a good storyteller, Thesis Tapes have the story of Joseph available on cassette. (Thesis Theological Cassettes, P.O. Box 11724, Pittsburgh, PA 15228.)
4. Print the names of the twelve tribes on twelve pieces of construction paper to correspond to the colors and shapes of the name tags. Put these around the room to designate meeting areas for the tribes.
5. Copy on newsprint the words of any of the songs you wish to use, if you do not purchase multiple copies for distribution.

PROCEDURE AND TIMING
Opening the gathering (30 minutes)

As persons arrive, give each one a tag so that no one

will have the same color or shape as others in his or her family. Ask them to print their own names in big letters, pin the tags on, and then to find others who belong to the same tribe (have the same color or shape).

After a few minutes of milling around, suggest that each tribe gather at the place designated by the signs which were placed around the room.

When the tribes are settled, give each tribe the appropriate card with Jacob's prediction on it. Ask each tribe to work together to introduce itself to the others in some creative, interesting way, using the description on the cards.

Call on each tribe in turn to "do their thing."

Developing the experience (30 minutes)

1. Have the song leader now teach the songs the group will sing. We suggest "Joseph's Coat" and the following bit from "Poor, Poor Joseph": "Poor, poor Joseph, what 'cha gonna do? Things look bad for you, hey, what'cha gonna do?" That is then repeated. The same tune is used for "Poor, poor Pharaoh, what'cha gonna do? Dreams are haunting you, hey, what'cha gonna do?"[1]

2. Introduce the story by playing "Jacob and Sons" on the record.

3. The group now sings "Joseph's Coat."

4. The storyteller tells about Joseph's dreams (Genesis 37:5-11) and the brothers' plan to get rid of Joseph (Genesis 37:12-20). At this point the group may sing "Poor, poor Joseph, what'cha gonna do?"

[1] Andrew Lloyd Webber and Tim Rice, *Joseph and the Amazing Technicolor Dreamcoat* (Dobbs Ferry, N.Y.: Novello & Co., Ltd.).

5. Storyteller continues with the selling of Joseph (Genesis 37:21-36). Omit the story of Judah and Tamar (chapter 38). Describe Joseph's work under Potiphar (Genesis 39:1-6) but omit the affair with Potiphar's wife (Genesis 39:7-23) and the interpretation of the prisoners' dreams (Genesis 40). Resume the story with the king's dream (Genesis 41). At the appropriate place, stop and have the group sing "Poor, poor Pharoah. . . ."

6. Tell briefly the rest of the story from Genesis 42-47, interspersing the narrative with music (recorded or sung) at any appropriate points which have been selected in advance.

7. Conclude the story by listening to the final song on the record "Any Dream Will Do" or by having the group sing again "Joseph's Coat."

8. Now ask the people to talk about the story in their tribes:
   • They can tell the parts of the story they liked best and least and why.
   • They can talk about the family member they identified with most.
   • They can talk about Jacob's family and their own family quarrels and reconciliations.

Closing the gathering (5 minutes)

Ask all the tribes to gather in a circle for a family reunion. Suggest that they sing in closing "Sisters, brothers, now it's time to part; Let us go in love, now, let us go in love" to the tune "Poor, Poor Joseph."

Elizabeth Gale is a free-lance writer who lives in King of Prussia, Pennsylvania.

FREEDOM IN THE FAMILY

by Elizabeth Wright Gale

GOAL: To affirm the worth of each individual in the family and to become aware of the conflict between the needs for freedom of each family member.

INTRODUCTION

Christian families are not free from conflict! In order to build a loving, caring relationship in the family, individuals must be willing to give up some personal freedom for the good of all.

PREPARATION
You will need:

1. Construction paper cut in fourths
2. Crayons and/or felt-tip markers
3. Pins

Things to do ahead of time

1. Set up as many tables as you think you will need for making name tags. In order to avoid a bottleneck, have enough so no more than twelve or fifteen persons will have to use one table.
2. Write instructions for name tags on large sheets of paper—one on each table. Tape these to the tables or to the wall near each table.
3. Secure a song leader (and pianist if you wish). Interpret the theme of the event to the song leader and make sure she or he has access to the suggested songs.
4. For the drama you will need seven people—a mother, a father, a grandmother, a girl of twelve, two boys, eleven and eight, and a narrator. They will need to rehearse the play "Don't Fence Me In." It will be most effective if the parts are memorized. If that is not practical, the drama can be presented as a play reading, but rehearsals will be needed so all players are very familiar with their lines, the setting, and the action.
5. Set up an area, perhaps a rug on the floor, where the group can gather for singing.
6. If the suggested songs are not well known, put the words on newsprint.
7. Arrange a section of the room for the drama. The first scene is in a dining room; the second in a living room. For the second scene you could push the dining table back, rearrange the chairs, and add a couple of floor pillows.
8. Decide on a method for forming the small groups so there are adults, youth, and children in each. This process should not take too much time; if it does, you will lose people's interest and some may wander off.

PROCEDURE AND TIMING
Opening the gathering (about 15 minutes)

As people arrive, direct them to the tables where they are to make name tags according to the following instructions which have been placed on or near each table.

1. Print your name in big letters at the top of the tag.
2. Under your name, draw or write something to show what freedom in the family means to you. One of the following sentence stems may help to get you started:

   I feel free when . . .
   If I were free, I would . . .
   Something which keeps me from feeling free is . . .
   I'm happy when I'm free to . . .

Developing the experience (45 to 60 minutes)

1. As soon as twelve or fifteen people have completed their name tags and pinned them on, it is time to begin the singing. This can be a flexible period with the number of songs used depending on the time you have. You might begin with a fun song, sung to the tune of "Three Blind Mice."

   Beautiful me, Beautiful you, (repeat)
   There is nothing that can ever surpass
   The beauty of a lad or lass

But beautiful me and beautiful you.
Beautiful us!

Other appropriate songs are: "Free to Be You and Me," "To Be Alive," "Glad to Be Me" (in *Come Sing with Me,* Judson Press, Valley Forge, Pennsylvania, and "Oh, Freedom."

2. Say a word to the total group about the theme of the program. If it is necessary for the people to move for the drama, ask them to do so now.
3. Introduce the drama and explain the plan for getting into small groups at its conclusion.
4. The drama group presents the play "Don't Fence Me In."
5. Repeat the instructions for getting into the small groups and assign gathering places. Give each group a card with the following directions.
   a. Share what each person in your group has written or drawn about freedom.
   b. Discuss the drama with these questions:
      1) What kinds of freedom did each member of the Bronson family wish to have?
      2) With which Bronson did you identify? Why?
      3) Which decisions do you think the children in the family should have been permitted to make? Why?
      4) What would you say is the main problem in the Bronson family?
      5) Is it possible for every member of a family to have complete freedom? Why?
   c. Write a new stanza for the song "Oh, Freedom" using the ideas of the group about freedom in the family.

Closing the gathering (about 10 minutes)

Ask each small group to sing their stanza of "Oh, Freedom." (It may help to have the pianist ready to accompany the groups.) If a group is reluctant to sing, ask if participants would read their words. If they are not ready to do that, go on to the next group.

Join in a big circle, hold hands, and sing the first stanza of the original "Oh, Freedom." The leader may conclude with the benediction: "Christ has set us free! Stand then, as free people" (Galatians 5:1*b*, TEV). Go in peace and freedom.

DON'T FENCE ME IN![1]

NARRATOR: We are presenting a skit in two scenes entitled, "Don't Fence Me In!" The action takes place in the Bronson home.

As you enter the house, you come into a hallway where there is a small table and a telephone. At the end of the hall is the back entrance to the house. To the right of the hall is the dining room.

The Bronson family includes Mother, who is constantly busy about household chores; Dad, who arrives each evening with a briefcase full of work to be done at home; Ted, who is eleven years old and will play baseball every chance he gets; Joyce, who is twelve years old, and who won't give anyone an opportunity to forget she is entering junior high school in September; Henry, who is eight years old, and a nuisance as far as Joyce is concerned; and, finally, Grandmother. She came to live with the Bronsons after Granddad's death a year ago.

¹ Fay DeBeck Flynt, "I Am Free?" *God Needs Me?* Christian Faith and Work Graded Series, Perspective I, Junior, Semester 2, Learner's Book (Valley Forge: American Baptist Board of Education and Publication, 1969), pp. 133-135. Used by permission of the American Baptist Board of Education and Publication.

Scene I takes place in the dining room. The table is set for six persons. When the scene opens, Mother is busy in the kitchen, Joyce is talking on the phone, and Henry has just come in from the outside.

HENRY: Dinner ready, Mom? I'm starved!

MOTHER: Yes, dear. Call the family. Dad will be here any minute.

HENRY: Joy-ceee! Mom says come and get it! Now! Pronto!

JOYCE: Hold on, Sally. *(sarcastically)* My dear little brother is calling me. (*To HENRY)* I'll come when I finish talking. Get lost!

HENRY: Okay, Miss Smarty.

NARRATOR: Dad arrives just in time to witness the loving byplay between brother and sister.

DAD: Are you two at it again? How many times have I told you to keep off each other's back!

HENRY: Don't blame me! I just told her dinner's ready, like Mom told me to. But she keeps right on yakking.

DAD *(sternly):* Joyce! Get off the phone immediately and give your mother some help in the kitchen.

JOYCE: Sally, I'll call back later. *(Replaces the receiver.)* I hate this family! Why can't I be left alone? You always embarrass me with my friends! I don't want any old dinner anyway!

MOTHER: Joyce, please help me to put the food on the table.

NARRATOR: Joyce goes off to help her mother, and Grandmother, Father, and Henry take their seats at the table.

GRANDMOTHER: Where's Ted?

HENRY: He's playing ball back of the Smiths' house. I saw him on my way home.

GRANDMOTHER: Not now. He's home. No one else can bang a door as loudly as he can!

TED: Hi, folks. Be with you in a sec. Got to. . . .

MOTHER *(cuts in on Ted):* Do you always have to cut it so close? How many times have I told you to be here at least fifteen minutes before dinner?

TED: I couldn't leave until the inning was over. We only had a couple of plays to go.

MOTHER: I don't care how many plays you had to go. When it's time to come home for dinner, you come home. Now sit down!

TED: Can't a guy make up his own mind about anything around here?

DAD: That's enough of that, Ted. Grandmother, will you please say grace?

(Everyone bows head for grace.)

NARRATOR: The "Amen" is hardly said when Dad commands,

DAD: Pass the chicken, Joyce.

NARRATOR: When the plate gets to Ted and Henry, they both try to spear the same piece of meat, and almost upset the platter.

MOTHER *(sharply):* Boys! There are two drumsticks. When will you ever learn to be polite to one another? Ted, you wait your turn.

GRANDMOTHER: The music on the radio is beautiful. Why don't we try to hear it?

NARRATOR: There is momentary silence as everyone eats. When dessert is distributed, mother issues what Ted calls her "O.F.E.'s"—orders for the evening.

MOTHER: Henry, will you please help Joyce with the dishes as soon as we finish eating?
Ted, will you please put away the hose and set out the trash cans? Tomorrow is trash collection day. *(Speaking to her husband)* And, Harold, will you see what you can do with that screen door? It won't latch properly.

DAD: Nancy, when I come home, I need a little freedom. I have a briefcase full of work I must get done before tomorrow morning. I won't have time to mend the door tonight.

MOTHER: Well! *You* need freedom? What do you think I need after washing, ironing, cooking, and cleaning all day? When do I get some freedom?

NARRATOR: While his parents are exchanging words, Ted decides it's a good time to slip out without being seen, or at least that's what he thinks. He forgets no one ever escapes his mother's eagle eye!

MOTHER: Ted! Where do you think you're going? I asked you to take care of those trash cans.

TED: Oh, Mom! I just want to see Pete a few minutes. I'll take care of the cans later.

MOTHER: You'll take care of the cans right now, young man. Later on you'll forget.

JOYCE: Mother, I don't have time to do the dishes tonight. Why can't Henry do them alone just once? I've got to get ready for Jane's party. The girls will be here for me any minute now.

MOTHER: After the dishes! If you get at them right away, it won't take long. You haven't told me who is coming by for you.

JOYCE: Mary and Helen.

MOTHER: Helen! I thought I've told you I don't like your going places with Helen. I don't understand why Jane's mother permits her to invite Helen.

JOYCE: Maybe Jane's mother gives her the freedom to pick her own friends, something I don't seem to have the right to do! Anyway, Helen is a lot of fun.

MOTHER: I'm advising you for your own good. Remember, Joyce, you're judged by the company you keep, and Helen's family doesn't have the best reputation in town.

GRANDMOTHER: I'm going to my room. Perhaps there I can be free from this turmoil!

NARRATOR: Scene 2 shifts to the living room. Mother, Father, and Henry are watching TV. Joyce comes downstairs as quietly as she can, hoping to get to the front door without being heard or seen. As did Ted, she forgets mothers have antennae which pick up sounds no one else hears.
Mother turns and is horrified at Joyce's appearance. She is wearing elaborate costume jewelry, and heavy eye makeup.

MOTHER: Joyce, where on earth did you get that stuff? You look like something from the comics!

JOYCE *(defiantly):* I bought it with *my* money!

MOTHER: I don't care whose money it was. It's a waste if you ask me.

JOYCE: Oh, Mother! All the girls in junior high school dress this way, and I'll be in junior high school in only two weeks! Anyway, why can't I dress as I please for my friend's party?

MOTHER *(wearily):* Oh, all right, skip it. But be home by 9:30.

JOYCE: Nine-thirty? The party won't be over by then. Besides, Jane's father is driving us home; we're not walking.

MOTHER: Okay, ten o'clock then.

JOYCE *(angrily):* Ted's right. This house is a jail. I can't talk to my friends on the phone. I can't wear clothes other girls wear. I can't spend my money as I want. I can't eat when I feel like it. I even have to go to sleep on schedule! Thank goodness I'm going to camp on Saturday. It'll give me a chance to get away from this old house!

NARRATOR: That's it, folks! The end of a pleasant evening in the Bronson home. Any resemblance to happenings in your home is purely intentional!

Elizabeth Gale is a free-lance writer who lives in King of Prussia, Pennsylvania.

ME IN MY FAMILY

by Elizabeth Wright Gale

GOAL: To recognize the contribution of each family member, to accept conflict as a normal part of family living, and to celebrate the uniqueness of each family.

INTRODUCTION

This session touches the subject of conflict in the family. Thomas Gordon, author of *Parent Effectiveness Training,* says, "How conflicts are resolved is probably the most critical factor in parent-child relationships." Families need to know that conflict is not to be avoided at any cost but is to be dealt with and used to bring about new understandings and closer relationships. Nuclear families will stay together for this session. Persons whose families are not with them may meet together in groups of six or eight.

PREPARATION
You will need:

1. Light-colored construction paper cut in half
2. Pencils, crayons or markers, pins
3. For each family, a copy of the two pictures "Family Quarrel" and "Family Group"
4. Paper for writing and drawing
5. Place some or all of the following supplies on a table or shelf: several packages of pipe cleaners, toothpicks, and bits of plastic foam such as is used for packing, straight pins and drinking straws, wire which can be bent easily but holds its shape

Things to do ahead of time

1. Make copies for each family of (a) directions for making the shields, (b) the questions for the picture study, (c) directions for writing the haiku poem, and (d) instructions about how to create a sculpture.
2. Make one or two song charts of "For Our Homes" and place them so the whole group will be able to see one of them.

For Our Homes[1]

3. Ask someone to be ready to lead the singing of the three songs.
4. It would be ideal for each family to be able to sit around a small table for this session. Or, they could sit in family groups on the floor. If you prefer tables, you might ask each family to bring a card table with them.

PROCEDURE AND TIMING
Opening the gathering (15–20 minutes)

1. Direct each family to find a table or spot which will be their "home" for the duration of the program.

[1] Lee Miller, *Crossroads,* Christian Faith and Work Graded Series, Perspective II, Middler, Semester 1 (Valley Forge: American Baptist Board of Education and Publication, 1970), p. 102. Used by permission of the American Baptist Board of Education and Publication.

Give them a copy of the directions for making the shields and enough construction paper for each person to make a shield.

> On your paper draw a shield to fill the paper. Add one vertical and one horizontal line through the center so there are four sections. Number the sections from left to right, top to bottom. Draw or write in the four sections of the shield the following:
> (1) The best thing about my family.
> (2) Something about my family I would like to change.
> (3) Something I contribute to my family.
> (4) Something my family values (thinks is important).
> Put your name on the paper outside the shield.

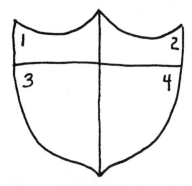

2. Sing together "People Need Each Other" (*Come Sing with Me,* Judson Press, Valley Forge, Pa.), and "He's Got the Whole World in His Hands," perhaps using the various family names, such as "He's got the Smith family in His hands." (You may wish to have the people move to a circle or to sit on a rug on the floor for the singing. However, do not take much time for moving; they could stay in their "home" areas.)

Developing the experience (45–60 minutes)

1. In their "home" areas family members share with each other what they have put on their shields. Urge people to listen to each other without defending or criticizing, to be open to learning something they had not known before, and to be willing to consider making changes which would benefit the whole family.

2. Give each family a copy of the two pictures and the following questions to be used as they study the pictures.

Picture Study

- What do you think might have caused each of the two scenes?
- Do you think the people in both pictures love and care for each other? Why?
- What might happen next?
- How does each picture make you feel?
- Make up a title for each picture.
- With which figures in the pictures do you identify most easily? Why?

3. Ask each family (not individuals) to compose a haiku poem about families. Give them pencils and paper and the following directions:
- line one, 5 syllables
- line two, 7 syllables
- line three, 5 syllables

4. Show the families where the supplies are for making the sculptures or drawings. They are to:
- Decide as a family the happiest time the family has ever had.
- Choose from the available supplies which they will use to portray their happiest time.

5. Arrange for two or three families to join together to share their poems, sculptures, or drawings.

Closing the gathering (5 minutes)

Form a circle to sing the prayer hymn "For Our Homes," using the song charts which were prepared in advance.

Elizabeth Gale is a free-lance writer who lives in King of Prussia, Pennsylvania.

Roger Lattner. Used with permission of Christian Board of Publication, St. Louis, MO.